Presented to:

_____

By:

_____

Date:

_____

Occasion:

_____

This book in its entirety—from literary development to artwork and final design—is a creation of Koechel Peterson & Associates. Artwork by Katia Andreeva is reproduced under license from Koechel Peterson & Associates and may not be reproduced without permission. For information regarding art prints featured in this book, please contact: Koechel Peterson & Associates, 2600 East 26th Street, Minneapolis, Minnesota, 55406, 1-612-721-5017.

Warner Faith

Time Warner Book Group
1271 Avenue of the Americas, New York, NY 10020
Visit our Web site at www.twbookmark.com

Printed in Singapore

ISBN: 0-446-57923-8

10 9 8 7 6 5 4 3 2 1

THE POWER
OF FORGIVENESS

CELEBRATION
OF SIMPLICITY

JOYCE MEYER

WARNER
Faith

New York • Boston • Nashville

THE POWER OF FORGIVENSS

CONTENTS

CELEBRATION OF SIMPLICITY

CONTENTS

THE POWER
OF FORGIVENESS

WHY WE
MUST
FORGIVE

Jesus taught us that we are to forgive those who hurt us, to pray for those who despitefully use us, and to bless those who curse us. That is hard. But there is something harder—being full of hatred, bitterness, and resentment.

GOD'S WORD FOR YOU

The Spirit of the Lord God is upon me, because the Lord has anointed and qualified me to preach the Gospel of good tidings to the meek, the poor, and afflicted; He has sent me to bind up and heal the brokenhearted, to proclaim liberty to the [physical and spiritual] captives and the opening of the prison and of the eyes to those who are bound . . .

ISAIAH 61:1

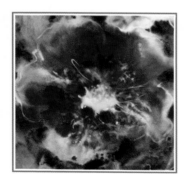

one

WHY WE MUST FORGIVE

Have you been hurt? Misused? Abused? Treated wrongly or improperly? Rejected? Has it affected your emotional state? Do you really want to be healed? Do you really want to get well? Will you forgive?

I believe that most people are abused in one way or another during their lifetime. It may come in the form of physical, verbal, emotional, or sexual abuse. Whatever form it takes, abuse causes a root of rejection, which is a devastating problem in our day.

I know all too much about this. I was sexually, physically, verbally, and emotionally abused from the time I can remember until I left home at the age of eighteen. I have been rejected, abandoned, betrayed, and divorced. I know what it means to hurt . . . and I thank God that He has shown me how to recover.

Wounded emotions can become a prison that locks us into our pain and keeps others out. Perhaps you are in the condition in life where I was, an emotional prisoner. It's a bitter, resentful, angry prison cell, and forgiveness is the key that unlocks the door that holds us there. How long have you been there? Do you want to be free of it?

Jesus came to open prison doors and to set the captives free! He wants to heal you. Jesus is willing; are you?

GOD'S WORD FOR YOU

There was a certain man there who had suffered with a deep-seated and lingering disorder for thirty-eight years.

When Jesus noticed him lying there [helpless], knowing that he had already been a long time in that condition, He said to him, Do you want to become well? [Are you really in earnest about getting well?]

JOHN 5:5–6

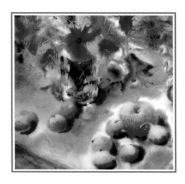

A QUESTION FOR THE HEART

For many, many years, "Why me, God?" was the cry of my heart, and it filled my thoughts and affected my attitude daily. I lived in the wilderness of self-pity, and it was a problem for me, my family, and the plan of God for my life. My troubled mind caused me to have a chip on my shoulder and to expect everyone else to fix my problem. I felt as though I was due something for the way I had been treated, but I was looking to people to pay me back when I should have been looking to God.

When Jesus addressed His question to the man who had been lying by the pool of Bethesda for thirty-eight years, He knew that self-pity would not deliver this man. "Do you want to become well?" are words of compassion to anyone who is trapped in an emotional prison and who has learned to function with their problem. They are words directed to the heart.

Gaining freedom from hurts and emotional bondages is not easy. I know. It will provoke feelings and emotions that have been "stuffed" rather than faced and dealt with. It may involve very real pain, but to be free and cleansed by the power of forgiveness is the only way to ever be fully well again.

God told me I could be pitiful or powerful, but I could not be both. I had to give up the self-pity to be free.

GOD'S WORD FOR YOU

In Him we have redemption (deliverance and salvation) through His blood, the remission (forgiveness) of our offenses (shortcomings and trespasses), in accordance with the riches and the generosity of His gracious favor,

Which He lavished upon us in every kind of wisdom and understanding (practical insight and prudence) . . .

EPHESIANS 1:7–8

PERSONAL SIN

To forgive those who have hurt us in the past is one of the ways we break the bondage of an emotional prison. But for many of us, dealing with our personal sin consciousness can also be a huge problem. The good news is that it doesn't have to be.

For a host of reasons that we will consider in this book, you may struggle with your sins in a way that you don't see in other believers' lives. When you sin or fail in any way, even when you make a mistake or display a weakness, you feel trapped there. You wonder if God is angry at you, and it's easy to doubt that He loves you. And you feel that you need to somehow atone for what you've done.

You know all the words about redemption and remission of our sins, and how God puts our sins away from Him as far as the east is from the west. But the faith to receive the gift of God's forgiveness doesn't seem to catch hold and work for you as it does for others.

I know about it. As a new believer, I would beg God's forgiveness for all my past sins every night. I wondered if I would ever find the peace I sought.

One evening as I prayed, I heard God say, "I forgave you the first time you asked, but you have not received My gift because you have not forgiven yourself."

GOD'S WORD FOR YOU

Asked by the Pharisees when the kingdom of God would come, He replied to them by saying, The kingdom of God does not come with signs to be observed or with visible display,

Nor will people say, Look! Here [it is]! or, See, [it is] there! For behold, the kingdom of God is within you [in your hearts] and among you [surrounding you].

LUKE 17:20–21

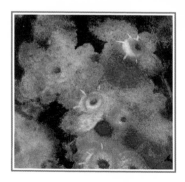

WHAT'S WRONG WITH ME?

For years in my Christian life I walked around with the nagging thought, *What's wrong with me?* Is that a question that troubles you as well?

I tried to do all the right things. My husband was an elder in the church, and I was on the evangelism committee and the church board. Our children went to parochial school. We didn't miss a church service, and I did everything I was told I should do to become spiritual. I tried and tried and tried, and yet it seemed that I just could not keep myself from making mistakes. I tried to earn righteousness by being good through the works of the flesh. And I ended up worn out, burned out, frustrated, and miserable.

It never occurred to me that I was suffering from years of abuse and rejection I had gone through. I thought that was all behind me. It was true that I was no longer being sexually abused, but it was all recorded in my emotions and my mind. I still had the effects of it, and I still acted them out. I needed to be healed emotionally, and I needed to forgive. I did not know the power of the kingdom of God within me.

I lived out of my own mind, will, and emotions, which were all damaged. Jesus had paid the price for my total deliverance, but I had no idea how to receive His gracious gift.

GOD'S WORD FOR YOU

You will fully recognize them by their fruits. Do people pick grapes from thorns, or figs from thistles?

Even so, every healthy (sound) tree bears good fruit [worthy of admiration], but the sickly (decaying, worthless) tree bears bad (worthless) fruit.

A good (healthy) tree cannot bear bad (worthless) fruit, nor can a bad (diseased) tree bear excellent fruit [worthy of admiration].

Every tree that does not bear good fruit is cut down and cast into the fire.

Therefore, you will fully know them by their fruits.

MATTHEW 7:16–20

BY YOUR FRUIT

The first thing to realize is that the fruit in our lives (our behavior) comes from somewhere. A person who is angry is that way for a reason. His behavior is the bad fruit of a bad tree with bad roots. It is important that we take a close and honest look at our fruit as well as our roots.

In my own life, there was a lot of bad fruit. I experienced regular bouts of depression, negativism, self-pity, quick temper, and the chip-on-the-shoulder syndrome. I had a controlling, domineering spirit. I was harsh, hard, rigid, legalistic, and judgmental. I held grudges and was fearful.

I worked hard at trying to correct it. Yet it seemed that no matter what kind of bad behavior I tried to get rid of, two or three others popped up somewhere else. It was like dandelions. I was not getting to the hidden root of the problem, and it would not die.

If this scenario sounds familiar to you, it may be that you have unresolved issues in your life that need to be searched out and removed so that everything can be made fresh and new. Don't run away. If God can change me, He certainly can change you.

Rotten fruit comes from rotten roots;
good fruit comes from good roots.

GOD'S WORD FOR YOU

For if you forgive people their trespasses [their reckless and willful sins, leaving them, letting them go, and giving up resentment], your heavenly Father will also forgive you.

But if you do not forgive others their trespasses [their reckless and willful sins, leaving them, letting them go, and giving up resentment], neither will your Father forgive you your trespasses.

MATTHEW 6:14–15

PROBLEMS PEOPLE MANIFEST

The fruit of unforgiveness creates a heart condition that is very dangerous, because the Bible tells us plainly that if we will not forgive other people, then God cannot forgive us. If we cannot forgive others, our faith doesn't work, and that has serious consequences.

Some people experience feelings of unworthiness. They have a shame-based self-hatred, a sense of self-rejection, and an inner voice that tells them they are no good, that something is wrong with them.

Other people become perfectionists. They are always trying to prove their worth and gain love and acceptance through performance. These people always struggle to do a little bit better in the hope that someone will love and accept them more.

Still others are supersensitive. Are you "touchy"? Would you like to be delivered from supersensitivity? If so, you need to face the fact that the problem is not with those who offend and hurt you, it is with you and your heart condition. Being secure will heal you of this.

Hatred, bitterness, resentment, loneliness, and addictions can be added to the list of bad fruit.

God has the marvelous ability to love us in the midst of our imperfections, and He wants to heal us. But in order for Him to do so, we must be willing to be helped.

GOD'S WORD FOR YOU

Go through, go through the gates! Prepare the way for the people. Cast up, cast up the highway! Gather out the stones. Lift up a standard or ensign over and for the peoples.

Behold, the Lord has proclaimed to the end of the earth: Say to the Daughter of Zion, Behold, your salvation comes [in the person of the Lord]; behold, His reward is with Him, and His work and recompense before Him.

And they shall call them the Holy People, the Redeemed of the Lord; and you shall be called Sought Out, a City Not Forsaken.

ISAIAH 62:10–12

PRETENDING

I was so miserable and unhappy. Yet, like so many people, I pretended that everything was fine. We human beings pretend for the benefit of others, not wanting them to know about our misery, but we also pretend for ourselves so that we do not have to face and deal with difficult issues.

Perhaps this describes you? I was one person on the inside and another on the outside. I pretended to be very confident, and in some ways I was. Still, I had very low self-esteem, and my so-called confidence was not really based on who I was in Christ. It was based on the approval of others, on my appearance and accomplishments, and on other external factors. Strip away the superficial exterior, and I was scared stiff. I was confused and full of inner turmoil.

The day came when I realized I had to face the truth and stop pretending. I don't think I ever realized just how miserable I was until I had spent some time in the Word of God and had begun to experience some emotional healing. If a person has never known true happiness, as was true of my life, how can he know what he is missing?

God will be your reward, and He will recompense you for what you have lost and what is missing.

GOD'S WORD FOR YOU

And we know (understand, recognize, are conscious of, by observation and by experience) and believe (adhere to and put faith in and rely on) the love God cherishes for us. God is love, and he who dwells and continues in love dwells and continues in God, and God dwells and continues in him.

In this [union and communion with Him] love is brought to completion and attains perfection with us, that we may have confidence for the day of judgment [with assurance and boldness to face Him], because as He is, so are we in this world.

There is no fear in love [dread does not exist], but full-grown (complete, perfect) love turns fear out of doors and expels every trace of terror! For fear brings with it the thought of punishment, and [so] he who is afraid has not reached the full maturity of love [is not yet grown into love's complete perfection].

We love Him, because He first loved us.

1 JOHN 4:16–19

STARVED FOR LOVE

We are created by God for love. Loving and being loved are what make life worth living. It gives life purpose and meaning. But if we have allowed sin and unforgiveness and the past to separate us from His love, it will leave us love-starved and unhappy.

Many people cannot maintain healthy, lasting relationships because either they don't know how to receive love or they place an unbalanced demand on others to give them what only God can give. The resulting frustration often leads to the ruin of marriages and the suffocation of friendships.

The Bible teaches us that God loves perfectly or unconditionally. His perfect love for us is not based on our perfection. It is not based on anything except Himself. God is Love (1 John 4:8). Love is Who He is. God always loves, but we often stop receiving His love.

God dealt with me for one solid year to get me to understand that He loves me unconditionally, not conditionally. I was unable to put my faith in His love because I was trapped in my unworthiness.

*The day of liberation finally came for me.
God graciously revealed to me, through the Holy Spirit,
His love for me personally. That single revelation
changed my entire life and walk with Him.*

GOD'S WORD FOR YOU

I am the Door; anyone who enters in through Me will be saved (will live). He will come in and he will go out [freely], and will find pasture.

The thief comes only in order to steal and kill and destroy. I came that they may have and enjoy life, and have it in abundance (to the full, till it overflows).

I am the Good Shepherd. The Good Shepherd risks and lays down His [own] life for the sheep.

JOHN 10:9–11

WALLS OF PROTECTION

After we have been hurt or felt the pain from rejection, it is our natural reaction to build elaborate defense systems of walls around our lives to protect our emotions from the same happening again. We put up an invisible (but real) wall between us and anyone who might be able to hurt us.

You see, Satan works in many different ways to steal your freedom and joy. These two go together! If Satan steals your freedom, he will also steal your joy. You will end up living in a little box, always trying to do what you think will be acceptable to everybody else . . . never being led by the Holy Spirit within you.

Self-made walls of protection never work. No one totally escapes rejection from others. Only God can build walls of protection around our lives, and it only happens by faith in His protection. We must allow the Holy Spirit to tear down the wrong walls so He can activate the protection of God that became available to us through salvation.

If you find yourself walled into your own little world, it's time to come out of your house and say, "I'm the King's kid! I'm going to walk without my walls! I'm believing God for a new start today! I will forgive."

RECEIVING FORGIVENESS

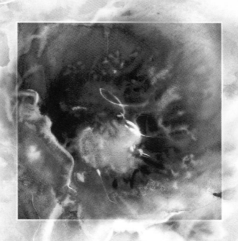

*Receiving forgiveness for past mistakes
and sins, and forgiving others for their
mistakes and sins, are two of the most
important and powerful factors in healing
our emotions and discovering
our freedom in Christ.*

GOD'S WORD FOR YOU

Jesus said to him, I am the Way and the Truth and the Life; no one comes to the Father except by (through) Me.

JOHN 14:6

But be doers of the Word [obey the message], and not merely listeners to it, betraying yourselves [into deception by reasoning contrary to the Truth].

JAMES 1:22

t w o

RECEIVING FORGIVENESS

 any people are hurting so badly, and they are crying out for help. The *problem* is, they are not willing to receive the help they need from God.

The *truth* is, no matter how much we may want or need help, we are never going to receive it until we are willing to do things God's way. It is amazing how many times we want help, but we want it *our* way.

In John 14:6, what Jesus meant when He said, "I am the Way," is that He has a certain way of doing things, and if we will submit to *His* way, everything will work out for us.

Matthew 6:14–15 says that if we forgive men when they sin against us, our heavenly Father will also forgive us. If we do not forgive men their sins, our heavenly Father will not forgive ours.

To receive from God what He has promised us in His Word, we must obey the Word, whether or not it is hard to act on it. Yes, we must receive the Word, but then we must become doers of the Word. We are not to wait to act according to our feelings.

God's way works! Forgiveness is a gift given to those who do not and will never deserve it. The power of forgiveness is the only way to freedom.

If we will do what we can, God will do what we can't.

GOD'S WORD FOR YOU

*So Jesus said to those Jews who had believed in Him,
If you abide in My word [hold fast to My teachings and
live in accordance with them], you are truly My disciples.*

*And you will know the Truth, and the Truth will set
you free.*

JOHN 8:31–32

*And when He comes, He will convict and convince
the world and bring demonstration to it about sin and
about righteousness (uprightness of heart and right standing
with God) and about judgment:*

*About sin, because they do not believe in Me [trust
in, rely on, and adhere to Me];*

*About righteousness (uprightness of heart and right
standing with God), because I go to My Father, and you
will see Me no longer . . .*

JOHN 16:8–10

Know the Truth

The Holy Spirit leads us through different steps to experience freedom in our lives. He guided me through the process while healing my emotions, which were damaged from years of abuse. I believe the Holy Spirit will guide you too as you seek to find victory and restoration of your broken spirit.

First, you must acknowledge the truth. You cannot be set free if you are living in denial. You cannot pretend either that certain negative things did not happen to you, or that you have not been influenced by them or reacted in response to them. Don't keep unforgiveness hidden away in a dark corner.

Ask the Holy Spirit to lead and guide you in this process. He convicts us of sin by exposing us to the truth that sets us free, but He never condemns us. He brings conviction so that we can see our errors, admit them, be truly sorry, repent, and receive forgiveness and cleansing in the precious blood of Jesus. The Holy Spirit has the power to break any bondage you may have, and He will enable you to walk free from what has been a sin in your life.

It is so wonderful to have Jesus as a friend, because He already knows everything about you. Why hide from Him? Come to Him and know you are loved and accepted no matter what is on your heart.

GOD'S WORD FOR YOU

Is anyone among you sick? He should call in the church elders (the spiritual guides). And they should pray over him, anointing him with oil in the Lord's name.

And the prayer [that is] of faith will save him who is sick, and the Lord will restore him; and if he has committed sins, he will be forgiven.

Confess to one another therefore your faults (your slips, your false steps, your offenses, your sins) and pray [also] for one another, that you may be healed and restored [to a spiritual tone of mind and heart]. The earnest (heartfelt, continued) prayer of a righteous man makes tremendous power available [dynamic in its working].

JAMES 5:14–16

Confess Your Faults

It is possible that you should consider putting James 5:16 into action. I think there is a place for eventually sharing with someone else if you are being tormented by your past sins. Being poisoned inwardly keeps you from getting well—physically, mentally, spiritually, or emotionally. There is something powerful about verbalizing it to another person that does wonders for us. That person can agree with you concerning your forgiveness and can even pray for you to be forgiven.

Once exposed to the light, things hidden in the dark lose their power. People hide things because of fear of what others would think if they knew. Numerous people have come to me for prayer, confiding in me, "I've never told this to anyone, but I feel I need to get it out of my system." Often they weep, and then a desperately needed release would come.

Use wisdom in whom you choose as a confidant. Ask God to lead you to a mature believer whom you can trust. It should be someone who is not going to be burdened down or harmed by what you share or use it to hurt you or make you feel worse about yourself.

The practice of confessing our faults to one another and receiving prayer is a powerful tool to help break bondages.

GOD'S WORD FOR YOU

*Behold, You desire truth in the inner being; make me
therefore to know wisdom in my inmost heart.*

PSALM 51:6

TELL YOURSELF THE TRUTH

God wants us to face the truth in our inmost being, then confess it in an appropriate manner to the right person. Sometimes the person who needs to hear the truth the most is us.

When people come to me for help in this area, I often tell them, "Go and look at yourself in the mirror and confess the problem to yourself."

If, for instance, your problem is that your parents did not love you as a child and you are resentful and bitter, face the facts as a reality once and for all. Look at yourself in the mirror and say, "My parents did not love me, and perhaps they never will."

Don't be one of those people who spend your life trying to get something you will never have. If you have let the fact that you were unloved ruin your life thus far, don't let it claim the rest of your life. Do what David did. Confess to yourself: "Although my father and my mother have forsaken me, yet the Lord will take me up [adopt me as His child]" (Psalm 27:10).

Whatever the problem may be that is bothering you, face it, consider confessing it to a trusted confidant, then admit it to yourself in your inmost being.

Admitting the truth causes the past to lose its grip on us.

GOD'S WORD FOR YOU

I, even I, am He Who blots out and cancels your transgressions, for My own sake, and I will not remember your sins.

ISAIAH 43:25

For as the heavens are high above the earth, so great are His mercy and loving-kindness toward those who reverently and worshipfully fear Him.

As far as the east is from the west, so far has He removed our transgressions from us.

As a father loves and pities his children, so the Lord loves and pities those who fear Him [with reverence, worship, and awe].

PSALM 103:11–13

RECEIVE YOUR FORGIVENESS

No matter what your problem or how bad you feel about yourself as a result of it, take this truth into your heart: God loves you. Jesus Christ gave His life that you might be forgiven, and He has given you a new life. God has given you a new family and new friends to love and accept and appreciate and support you. You are going to make it because of the One Who lives inside you and cares for you.

Confess to God whatever it is that stands between Him and you as sin. No matter what you may have done, say, "Lord, I did it, and it is a marvel to me to realize that I can stand here and look myself in the eye. But I can do so because I know that, even though what I did was wrong, You have put my sins as far away from me as the east is from the west, and You remember them no more!"

Once you have confessed your sins and asked for God's forgiveness, if you continue to drag them up to Him every time you go to Him in prayer, you are reminding Him of something He has not only *forgiven* but also actually *forgotten*.

*From this moment, stop punishing yourself
for something that no longer exists.*

GOD'S WORD FOR YOU

In Him we have redemption (deliverance and salvation) through His blood, the remission (forgiveness) of our offenses (shortcomings and trespasses), in accordance with the riches and the generosity of His gracious favor . . .

EPHESIANS 1:7

You were bought with a price [purchased with a preciousness and paid for, made His own]. So then, honor God and bring glory to Him in your body.

1 CORINTHIANS 6:20

PURCHASED BY JESUS' BLOOD

Say aloud to yourself, "I was bought and cleansed from sin with a price; purchased with a preciousness; paid for and made God's own."

We are delivered from sin and all the "death" it brings with it. Worry, anxiety, and fear are forms of death. Strife, bitterness, resentment, and unforgiveness are forms of death. The blood of Jesus is the only antidote for death.

Jesus' blood is precious before the Father and should be precious to us. A precious thing is something we protect, something we are careful with, something we don't want to part with. The blood of Jesus is precious, and it should be honored and respected.

The blood of Jesus cleanses us from sin and will continuously cleanse us (1 John 1:9). His blood is like a powerful cleansing agent. Just as our blood works to keep our bodies cleansed of all poison, the blood of Jesus continuously cleanses us from sin in all its forms and manifestations.

Repentance releases the power of the blood of Jesus in your behalf. Let the Lord "wash" you in the blood. Release your faith in the blood of Jesus.

GOD'S WORD FOR YOU

Therefore, [there is] now no condemnation (no adjudging guilty of wrong) for those who are in Christ Jesus, who live [and] walk not after the dictates of the flesh, but after the dictates of the Spirit.

ROMANS 8:1

GUILT AND CONDEMNATION

One of the major problems for many believers is the recurrence of feeling guilty and condemned for past sins that they have received forgiveness for. Satan's great delight is to make us feel bad about ourselves, and one way to do that is by telling us our forgiveness wasn't complete.

The Bible teaches that through the blood of Jesus we have complete forgiveness and total freedom from condemnation. We don't need to add our guilt to His sacrifice upon the cross. He is more than enough.

If the devil tries to bring that sin to your mind again in the form of guilt and condemnation, declare to him: "I was forgiven for that sin! It has been taken care of; therefore, I take no care for it." You will find that speaking aloud is often helpful to you because by doing so you are declaring your stand on the Word of God. Declare to the principalities and powers that Christ has set you free.

Don't just sit and listen to the devil's accusations and lies. Learn to talk back to him with the truth. Begin to see yourself as the righteousness of God in Christ Jesus.

GOD'S WORD FOR YOU

Therefore I will not restrain my mouth; I will speak in the anguish of my spirit, I will complain in the bitterness of my soul [O Lord]!

JOB 7:11

FORGIVING GOD

Many people have problems of unforgiveness toward God. Those who have never experienced that feeling may not understand it. But those who have know what it is to feel animosity toward God because they blame Him for cheating them out of something important in their lives. Things have not worked out the way they had planned. They figure that God could have changed things if He had wanted to, but since He didn't, they feel disappointed and blame Him for their situation.

If you are holding on to this attitude, you know it is impossible to have fellowship with someone you are mad at. If so, the only answer is to forgive God. Of course, God does not need to be forgiven! But such heart honesty can break the bondage and restore the fellowship that has been broken with the Lord.

Often we think if we just knew *why* certain things happened to us, we would be satisfied. I believe God tells us only what we really need to know, what we are prepared to handle, and what will not harm us, but will, in fact, help us. We must learn to trust God and not try to figure out everything in life.

There must come a time when we stop living in the past and asking why. Instead, we must learn to let God turn our scars into stars.

GOD'S WORD FOR YOU

And this is the message [the message of promise] which we have heard from Him and now are reporting to you: God is Light, and there is no darkness in Him at all [no, not in any way].

[So] if we say we are partakers together and enjoy fellowship with Him when we live and move and are walking about in darkness, we are [both] speaking falsely and do not live and practice the Truth [which the Gospel presents].

1 JOHN 1:5–6

OPENING UP TO GOD

The power of forgiveness frees us from all guilt and condemnation and allows us to come out of the darkness into the light of God (1 John 1:5–6). So often in the past we tried to hide things by burying them deep inside our own darkness. But in God there is no darkness at all. So when we allow Him full entrance into our hearts and minds, there is no darkness.

I am so glad that God fills every room of my heart with His light. There are no places in my heart that I know of that are blocked off from Him and the light that comes from His presence.

We must allow the Lord to come into the dark recesses of the heart and fill them with His marvelous light. We need to open ourselves to the searching, cleansing light of the Holy Spirit of God. The result is that while we used to live and walk in darkness and fear and misery, now we can live and walk in light and peace and joy. God will fill every part of our lives with His life-giving Spirit so that we can live free!

What a great feeling to get rid of the pretending.
No more putting on a facade and playing games.
It feels great to walk in the light!

FORGIVING
OTHERS

God has new plans on the horizon of your life, but you will never see them if you live with unforgiveness in your heart.

GOD'S WORD FOR YOU

But He gives us more and more grace (power of the Holy Spirit, to meet this evil tendency and all others fully). That is why He says, God sets Himself against the proud and haughty, but gives grace [continually] to the lowly (those who are humble enough to receive it).

JAMES 4:6

three

FORGIVING OTHERS

have read that medical studies indicate that 75 percent of physical sickness is caused by emotional problems. And one of the greatest emotional problems people experience is guilt. Many people are punishing themselves with sickness. They are refusing to relax and enjoy life because, after all, they don't *deserve* to have a good time. So they live in perpetual penance of regret and remorse. This kind of stress makes people sick.

There are two things that cause us to get all knotted up inside. The first is the negative things done to us by others. The second is the negative things we have done to ourselves and others. We have a hard time getting over what others have done to us, and we find it difficult to forget what we have done to ourselves and others.

Many years ago I had a choice to remain bitter, full of hatred and self-pity, resenting the people who had hurt and abused me as well as those who were able to enjoy nice, normal lives, those who had never been hurt as I was. Or, I could choose to follow God's path, allowing Him to make me a better person because of what I had been through. I thank Him that He gave me the grace to make it through and follow His way rather than Satan's way.

God's way is forgiveness.

GOD'S WORD FOR YOU

*Then he answered and spake unto me, saying,
This is the word of the LORD unto Zerubbabel, saying,
Not by might, nor by power, but by my spirit, saith the
LORD of hosts.*

ZECHARIAH 4:6 KJV

They who sow in tears shall reap in joy and singing.

PSALM 126:5

DOORWAYS OF PAIN

For many of us, forgiving someone who has hurt us is the most difficult part of emotional healing. It can even be the stumbling block that prevents it. Those who have been badly wounded by others know that it is much easier to say the word *forgive* than it is to do it.

First, let me say that it is not possible to have good emotional health while harboring bitterness, resentment, and unforgiveness toward someone. It's poison to your system. And it is impossible to get better if it's there.

When I finally allowed the Lord to begin to work in my life, He revealed to me I had been hiding behind "doorways of pain"—the painful events and situations of my past. To pass back through the same, or similar, doorways and be delivered and healed meant facing the issues, people, and truths I found so difficult, if not impossible, to face on my own.

Don't be afraid of the pain. The temptation is to run away, but the Lord says that we are to go through our problems. Let your pain lead you out of bondage, not deeper into it. Endure whatever you need to, knowing that there is joy on the other side.

God does not bring hurts and wounds upon us.
But if they are inflicted upon us,
He is able to make miracles out of mistakes.

GOD'S WORD FOR YOU

Let all bitterness and indignation and wrath (passion, rage, bad temper) and resentment (anger, animosity) and quarreling (brawling, clamor, contention) and slander (evil-speaking, abusive or blasphemous language) be banished from you, with all malice (spite, ill will, or baseness of any kind).

And become useful and helpful and kind to one another, tenderhearted (compassionate, understanding, loving-hearted), forgiving one another [readily and freely], as God in Christ forgave you.

EPHESIANS 4:31–32

If you forgive anyone anything, I too forgive that one; and what I have forgiven, if I have forgiven anything, has been for your sakes in the presence [and with the approval] of Christ (the Messiah),

To keep Satan from getting the advantage over us; for we are not ignorant of his wiles and intentions.

2 CORINTHIANS 2:10–11

BE QUICK TO FORGIVE

The Bible teaches us to forgive "readily and freely." That is His standard for us, no matter how we feel about it. We are to be quick to forgive.

According to 1 Peter 5:5, we are to clothe ourselves with the character of Jesus Christ, meaning that we are to be long-suffering, patient, not easily offended, slow to anger, quick to forgive, and filled with mercy.

My definition of "mercy" is the ability to look beyond what is done to discover the reason why it was done. Many times people do things even they don't understand themselves, but there is always a reason why people behave as they do.

The same is true of us as believers. We are to be merciful and forgiving, just as God in Christ forgives us our wrongdoing—even when we don't understand why we do what we do.

The choice to forgive others is ours. He will not force anyone to do it. Even if you don't understand it, choose to follow it, believing that God's way is the best. It works. He can take what Satan meant to destroy you and turn it to your good. You must believe that or you will despair (Psalm 27:13).

We are to forgive in order to keep Satan from getting the advantage over us.

GOD'S WORD FOR YOU

Exercise foresight and be on the watch to look [after one another], to see that no one falls back from and fails to secure God's grace (His unmerited favor and spiritual blessing), in order that no root of resentment (rancor, bitterness, or hatred) shoots forth and causes trouble and bitter torment, and the many become contaminated and defiled by it . . .

HEBREWS 12:15

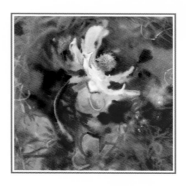

A ROOT OF BITTERNESS

When we allow unforgiveness in our lives, we are filled with resentment and bitterness. *Bitterness* refers to something that is pungent or sharp to the taste.

We remember that when the children of Israel were about to be led out of Egypt, they were told by the Lord on the eve of their departure to prepare a Passover meal that included bitter herbs. Why? God wanted them to eat those bitter herbs as a reminder of the bitterness they had experienced in bondage. Bitterness always goes hand in hand with bondage.

How does bitterness get started? It grows from a root, which *The King James Version* speaks of as a *root of bitterness*. A root of bitterness from the seed of unforgiveness always produces the fruit of bitterness.

Bitterness results from the many minor offenses we just can't let go of, the things we rehearse over and over inside us until they have become blown way out of proportion. And it comes from the major offenses people commit against us. The longer we allow them to grow and fester, the more powerful they become.

*A root of bitterness will infect our entire being —
our personality, our attitude and behavior,
our perspective, and our relationships,
especially our relationship with God.*

GOD'S WORD FOR YOU

And you shall hallow the fiftieth year and proclaim liberty throughout all the land to all its inhabitants. It shall be a jubilee for you . . .

And if your brother becomes poor beside you and sells himself to you, you shall not compel him to serve as a bondman (a slave not eligible for redemption).

But as a hired servant and as a temporary resident he shall be with you; he shall serve you till the Year of Jubilee,

And then he shall depart from you, he and his children with him, and shall go back to his own family and return to the possession of his fathers.

LEVITICUS 25:10, 39–41

And whenever you stand praying, if you have anything against anyone, forgive him and let it drop (leave it, let it go), in order that your Father Who is in heaven may also forgive you your [own] failings and shortcomings and let them drop.

MARK 11:25

LET IT GO!

Do yourself a favor and let the offense and the offender go! To forgive is to keep yourself from being poisoned and imprisoned. To forgive is to excuse or pardon a fault or offense.

When a person is found guilty of a crime and sentenced to prison, we say he owes a debt to society. But if he is pardoned, he is allowed to go his way freely with no restraints upon him. Such a pardon cannot be earned, it must be granted by a higher authority.

When someone hurts us, we react as though that individual has stolen something from us. We feel they owe us. Yet Jesus told us we should let it go. We should drop it. And He taught us to pray in the Lord's Prayer, "Forgive us our debts, as we forgive our debtors."

In Leviticus 25 we read about the Year of Jubilee in which all debts were forgiven and all debtors were pardoned and set free in Israel. When we are in Christ, every day can be a Year of Jubilee if we are willing.

It is time to release that person from their debt and let it and them go. It is time to allow the Year of Jubilee to be celebrated in our lives.

The good news of the Cross is that Jesus paid the debt for us. God can say to us, "You don't owe Me anything anymore!"

GOD'S WORD FOR YOU

Then Jesus said to them again, Peace to you! [Just] as the Father has sent Me forth, so I am sending you.

And having said this, He breathed on them and said to them, Receive the Holy Spirit!

[Now having received the Holy Spirit, and being led and directed by Him] if you forgive the sins of anyone, they are forgiven; if you retain the sins of anyone, they are retained.

JOHN 20:21–23

RECEIVE THE HOLY SPIRIT'S HELP

The number one rule in forgiving sin is to receive the Holy Spirit, Who provides the strength and ability to forgive. None of us can do that on our own.

In John 20, I believe when Jesus breathed on the disciples and they received the Holy Spirit, they were born again at that moment. The next thing He said to them was that whatever sins they forgave were forgiven and whatever sins they retained were retained. The forgiving of sins seems to be the first power conferred upon people when they become born again. If that is so, then the forgiving of sins is our first duty as believers.

After realizing that you cannot forgive apart from the Holy Spirit's help, pray and release the person who hurt you. Repeat this prayer aloud: "Holy Spirit, breathe on me and give me strength. I forgive (name) for (whatever was done to you). I loose this person from their debt. I choose to walk in Your ways, Lord. I love You, and I turn this situation over to You. I cast my care upon You, and I believe You for my total restoration. Help me, Lord. Heal me of all the wounds inflicted upon me."

Now by faith leave it all in your Father's hands.

On our journey to wholeness, we are usually all knotted up inside. As we forgive, Jesus begins to straighten up our lives by untying one knot at a time.

GOD'S WORD FOR YOU

You have heard that it was said, You shall love your neighbor and hate your enemy;

But I tell you, Love your enemies and pray for those who persecute you . . .

MATTHEW 5:43–44

Invoke blessings upon and pray for the happiness of those who curse you, implore God's blessing (favor) upon those who abuse you [who revile, reproach, disparage, and high-handedly misuse you].

LUKE 6:28

Bless those who persecute you [who are cruel in their attitude toward you]; bless and do not curse them.

ROMANS 12:14

BLESS, NOT CURSE

Do you see what is missing when we just forgive someone and go no further? God in His Word instructs us to *forgive* others and then to *bless* them.

In this context, the word *bless* means "to speak well of." It is extending mercy to people who do not deserve it. And we are to pray for them to be blessed spiritually. We are to ask God to bring truth and revelation to them about their attitude and behavior so they will be willing to repent and be set free from their sins.

Revenge says, "You mistreated me, so I will mistreat you." Mercy says, "You mistreated me, so I'm going to forgive you, restore you, and treat you as if you never hurt me." What a blessing to be able to give and receive mercy. Give mercy and you will receive mercy.

Mercy is an attribute of God that is seen in how He deals with His people. Mercy is good to us when we deserve judgment. Mercy accepts and blesses us when we deserve to be totally rejected. Mercy understands our weaknesses and does not judge us.

The power of forgiveness will never work if we say we forgive but then turn around and curse the offender with our tongues or rehash the offense with others.

GOD'S WORD FOR YOU

Do not be unequally yoked with unbelievers [do not make mismated alliances with them or come under a different yoke with them, inconsistent with your faith]. For what partnership have right living and right standing with God with iniquity and lawlessness? Or how can light have fellowship with darkness?

What harmony can there be between Christ and Belial [the devil]? Or what has a believer in common with an unbeliever?

2 CORINTHIANS 6:14–15

ℱORGIVENESS AND RESTORATION

Many people have the mistaken idea that if someone has hurt them and they forgive that person, they will have to go back and suffer through the same hurt all over again. They think that in order to forgive, they must enter back into an active relationship with the person who has injured them. That is not true, and this misconception has caused a problem for many people who want to forgive.

Forgiveness does not necessarily mean restoration. If the relationship can be restored, and it is within God's will for it to be restored, then restoration is the best plan. But a broken relationship cannot always be restored. Sometimes it would not even be wise, especially in cases where abuse has been involved. It may even be dangerous.

In my own case, although I forgave my father who abused me and eventually tried to have fellowship with him, he made it clear he did not think he had ever done anything wrong. In fact, although he has now repented, at that time he went so far as to blame me for what happened. Without repentance on his part, that relationship could not have been reconciled.

Don't get caught in a trap that will open your wound and cause it to start bleeding again.

GOD'S WORD FOR YOU

Be still and rest in the Lord; wait for Him and patiently lean yourself upon Him; fret not yourself because of him who prospers in his way, because of the man who brings wicked devices to pass.

Cease from anger and forsake wrath; fret not yourself—it tends only to evildoing.

PSALM 37:7–8

It shall be said in that day, Behold our God upon Whom we have waited and hoped, that He might save us! This is the Lord, we have waited for Him; we will be glad and rejoice in His salvation.

ISAIAH 25:9

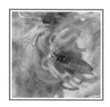

*F*ORGIVENESS VERSUS FEELINGS

I believe that the greatest deception in the area of forgiveness Satan has perpetuated in the church is the idea that if a person's feelings have not changed, he has not forgiven. Many people believe this deception. They decide to forgive someone who has harmed them, but the devil convinces them that because they still have the same feelings toward the person, they have not fully forgiven that individual.

You can make all the correct decisions and for a long time not "feel" any different from the way you felt before you decided to forgive. This is where faith is needed to carry you through. You have done your part and now you are waiting for God to do His. His part is to heal your emotions, to make you feel well and not wounded. Only God has the power to change your feelings toward the person who hurt you.

Waiting is where the battle is won in the spiritual realm. Waiting and keeping your eyes on God will put pressure on the demonic forces that initiated the problem to begin with, and they have to give back the ground they had gained. Healing takes time!

You can make a decision to obey God, but you can't change how you feel. God will do that over time.

RESTORING THE SOUL

For change to be lasting, it must come from the inside out. Only God can cause that type of heart change. Let God be God.

GOD'S WORD FOR YOU

The Lord is my Shepherd [to feed, guide, and shield me], I shall not lack.

He makes me lie down in [fresh, tender] green pastures; He leads me beside the still and restful waters.

He refreshes and restores my life (my self); He leads me in the paths of righteousness [uprightness and right standing with Him—not for my earning it, but] for His name's sake.

PSALM 23:1–3

four
RESTORING THE SOUL

The Twenty-third Psalm is so comforting. In it the psalmist David tells us it is the Lord Who leads us, Who feeds, guides, and shields us. Who causes us to lie down and rest, Who refreshes and restores our soul.

It is through the power of forgiveness that God leads us in the paths of righteousness, uprightness, and right standing with Him. David is saying that God leads each of us in the path right for us individually. If we will allow Him to do so, He will guide us by His Holy Spirit into the unique path that leads to the fulfillment of His planned destiny for us.

Through the doorway of forgiveness, God refreshes and restores our soul or our life. It is with our soul that our body contacts the world, primarily through our personality, and it is with our spirit that we contact God. *Webster's Dictionary* tells us that the word *restore* means: "1. To bring back into existence or use. 2. To bring back to an original state. 3. To put back in a former position. 4. To make restitution of: give back."

God promises restoration of what was lost or ruined through unforgiveness. I can verify He keeps His promises.

You have a blood-bought right to enjoy your life. Be determined to keep the power of forgiveness working its freedom in your life.

GOD'S WORD FOR YOU

For we are God's [own] handiwork (His workmanship), recreated in Christ Jesus, [born anew] that we may do those good works which God predestined (planned beforehand) for us [taking paths which He prepared ahead of time], that we should walk in them [living the good life which He prearranged and made ready for us to live].

EPHESIANS 2:10

For I know the thoughts and plans that I have for you, says the Lord, thoughts and plans for welfare and peace and not for evil, to give you hope in your final outcome.

JEREMIAH 29:11

God's Predestined Plan

God had a good plan laid out for each of us before we made our appearance on this planet. God's unique plan for each of us is not a plan of failure, misery, poverty, sickness, and disease. His plan is a good plan, a plan for life and health, happiness, and fulfillment.

In John 10:10 Jesus said, "The thief comes only in order to steal and kill and destroy. I came that they may have and enjoy life, and have it in abundance." The devil comes to disrupt that plan and to destroy the good thing God has in mind for us.

God's good plan may have been disrupted in our lives, but we need to understand His heart and the restorative power of His forgiveness. He doesn't like it when someone hurts us and tries to undermine His plan for us. It should be a great comfort to us to know that while He is making us lie down in green pastures to restore our soul, He is working on our behalf concerning our situation!

If we will trust the Lord, He will do for us what we cannot do for ourselves. Only He has the power to restore what has been lost to us, whether that loss was our fault or the fault of our enemy.

GOD'S WORD FOR YOU

But the Comforter (Counselor, Helper, Intercessor, Advocate, Strengthener, Standby), the Holy Spirit, Whom the Father will send in My name [in My place, to represent Me and act on My behalf], He will teach you all things. And He will cause you to recall (will remind you of, bring to your remembrance) everything I have told you.

JOHN 14:26

MEMORIES

The basic meaning of the word *restore* is "to turn back (hence, away) . . . literally or figuratively (not necessarily with the idea of return to the starting point)." God wants to take us back to the point of departure, the place where we veered from His plan for us, then bring us forward to make things work out the way He intended from the beginning. He will not necessarily take us back to the place physically, and often does not. I don't think He even wants us to try to go there in our memory and relive that experience, although perhaps some people need to do that if there is a memory that has been blocked and needs to be faced.

There are things about my childhood I cannot recall, and it doesn't bother me a bit. Some things are better off not being remembered or relived. Many times a God-given ability to forget is a real blessing.

One facet of the ministry of the Holy Spirit is to bring things to our remembrance. Rather than digging into our past, we must trust God to bring only the right things to our attention.

It is dangerous to go back into your subconscious and dig up all kinds of harmful and hurtful memories. Trust the Holy Spirit to bring forth only those things that need to be dealt with.

GOD'S WORD FOR YOU

When Joseph had come to his brothers, they stripped him of his [distinctive] long garment which he was wearing;

Then they took him and cast him into the [well-like] pit which was empty; there was no water in it.

GENESIS 37:23–24

And Pharaoh said to Joseph, Forasmuch as [your] God has shown you all this, there is nobody as intelligent and discreet and understanding and wise as you are.

You shall have charge over my house, and all my people shall be governed according to your word [with reverence, submission, and obedience]. Only in matters of the throne will I be greater than you are.

GENESIS 41:39–40

From the Pit to the Palace

A pit is a ditch, a trap, or a snare. It refers to destruction. Satan always wants to bring us into the pit.

Joseph was sold into slavery by his brothers who hated him. They actually threw him into a pit and intended to leave him there to die, but God had other plans. He ended up being sold into slavery in Egypt, where he was abused and ended up in prison for refusing to compromise his integrity. Yet everywhere Joseph went, God gave him favor. Ultimately, he ended up in the palace, second in command to Pharaoh.

How did Joseph get from the pit to the palace? I believe it was by remaining positive, refusing to be bitter, and being confident and trusting God. Even though it looked like he was defeated on many occasions, he kept standing up on the inside.

Joseph had a right attitude. Without a right attitude, a person can start in the palace and end up in a pit, which actually happens to a lot of people. Some, it seems, have great opportunities given to them, and they do nothing with their lives, while others who get a very bad start in life overcome all obstacles and succeed.

No matter where you started, you can have a great finish! I challenge you to do something great for God.

GOD'S WORD FOR YOU

As for you, you thought evil against me, but God meant it for good, to bring about that many people should be kept alive, as they are this day.

GENESIS 50:20

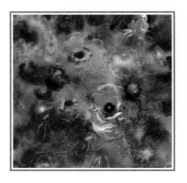

Good from Bad

God wants to restore your soul. One way or another, He wants to go back to where your life got off track and make everything right from that moment forward.

Joseph is the classic biblical example of how God takes what was meant for evil against us and works it out for our good. In that dramatic scene where Joseph is speaking in Genesis 50:20, he tells his brothers that what they meant to him as evil, and was truly evil, God had used for good to save them and their families and hundreds of thousands of others in a time of famine.

In my own life, I cannot truthfully say I am glad I was abused. But through the power of forgiveness and yielding my abuse to God, He has healed me and made me a better, stronger, more spiritually powerful and sensitive person. He has restored my soul and driven out the fear and insecurity. I can trust, love, forgive, and live with simplicity in my approach to life. I am free to enjoy what I do.

Only God can bring good from bad.

Although even the Lord cannot change what has happened to you, He can change the consequences of it.

GOD'S WORD FOR YOU

The Spirit of the Lord God is upon me, because the Lord has anointed and qualified me to preach the Gospel of good tidings to the meek, the poor, and afflicted; He has sent me to bind up and heal the brokenhearted, to proclaim liberty to the [physical and spiritual] captives and the opening of the prison and of the eyes to those who are bound,

To proclaim the acceptable year of the Lord [the year of His favor] and the day of vengeance of our God, to comfort all who mourn,

To grant [consolation and joy] to those who mourn in Zion—to give them an ornament (a garland or diadem) of beauty instead of ashes, the oil of joy instead of mourning, the garment [expressive] of praise instead of a heavy, burdened, and failing spirit—that they may be called oaks of righteousness [lofty, strong, and magnificent, distinguished for uprightness, justice, and right standing with God], the planting of the Lord, that He may be glorified.

ISAIAH 61:1–3

OPENING THE ASHES

Here in Isaiah 61:3 we are told that as part of His restoration process, the Lord gives beauty for ashes. But for that to happen to us, we must be willing to give Him the ashes.

You may have been hurt in the past and have kept the ashes of that hurt somewhere close at hand. Every once in a while you may get them out and re-grieve over them. If so, I understand because I used to do the same thing.

But you need to do what I did and let go of these ashes, allowing the wind of the Holy Spirit to blow them away to where they cannot be found again. This is a new day. There is no more time left for grieving over the ashes of the past. You have no future dwelling in your past.

God has the same good plan for you that He had the moment you arrived on this planet. He has never changed His mind, and He never will. From the very moment the enemy hurt you, God has had your restoration in His heart. Know that you are valuable, unique, loved, and special in His eyes!

Allow the Holy Spirit to blow away the ashes
that are left behind from Satan's attempt to destroy you
and replace those ashes with beauty.

GOD'S WORD FOR YOU

Yes, though I walk through the [deep, sunless] valley of the shadow of death, I will fear or dread no evil, for You are with me; Your rod [to protect] and Your staff [to guide], they comfort me.

You prepare a table before me in the presence of my enemies. You anoint my head with oil; my [brimming] cup runs over.

Surely or only goodness, mercy, and unfailing love shall follow me all the days of my life, and through the length of my days the house of the Lord [and His presence] shall be my dwelling place.

PSALM 23:4–6

My Cup Runneth Over!

I love the words in the last part of David's most beloved hymn of praise to God in Psalm 23. He describes the condition the Lord wants us to be in constantly. He wants us to be protected, guided, and comforted. He wants to set a table of blessings before us in the very face of our enemies. He wants to anoint us with the oil of joy instead of mourning. He wants our cup of blessings to overflow continually in thanksgiving and praise to Him for His goodness, mercy, and unfailing love toward us. And He wants us to live forever, moment by moment, in His Holy presence.

All these "wants" are a part of His good plan for each of us. Regardless of how far we may have fallen, He wants to raise us up and restore us to that right and perfect plan He has for our lives.

It would benefit every one of us if we would say to ourselves several times a day, "God has a fantastic plan for my life. I want all that He wants for me. I receive His anointing of the Holy Spirit to fill my cup and overflow. I will walk and live in the presence of the Lord."

*Remember that the most important thing
in receiving God's blessings is not our great faith
but His great faithfulness.*

GOD'S WORD FOR YOU

You shall not need to fight in this battle; take your positions, stand still, and see the deliverance of the Lord [Who is] with you. . . . Fear not nor be dismayed. Tomorrow go out against them, for the Lord is with you.

And Jehoshaphat bowed his head with his face to the ground, and all Judah and the inhabitants of Jerusalem fell down before the Lord, worshiping Him.

And some Levites . . . stood up to praise the Lord, the God of Israel, with a very loud voice.

And they rose early in the morning and went out into the Wilderness of Tekoa; and as they went out, Jehoshaphat stood and said, Hear me, O Judah . . . Believe in the Lord your God and you shall be established; believe and remain steadfast to His prophets and you shall prosper.

When he had consulted with the people, he appointed singers to sing to the Lord and praise Him in their holy [priestly] garments as they went out before the army, saying, Give thanks to the Lord, for His mercy and loving-kindness endure forever!

2 CHRONICLES 20:17–21

$\mathscr{R}$ESTORED TO WORSHIP

Through the power of forgiveness we enter into God's rest and take our position in Jesus Christ. We find that He is our peace, our justification, and our provider. It is the joy of the Lord that is our strength. He does not just give us joy; He is our joy and our hope. We are to abide in Jesus and bless and worship Him.

Worship transforms us. By starting to worship God for the changes that He is already working in us, we find that those changes start manifesting more and more, and we experience new levels of God's glory, which is the manifestation of all His excellencies. In other words, God will pour His goodness out upon the worshiper.

There is a release that comes through worship. Sometimes we need a mental or emotional release. As we worship the Lord, we release our emotional or mental burden that is weighing us down. It is swallowed up in the awesomeness of God.

Begin to worship early in the morning. Worship while you are getting ready for work, and when you are on your way to work. You will be amazed to see how things begin to change at home and on the job.

Worship creates an atmosphere where God can work.

GOD'S WORD FOR YOU

I thank God Whom I worship with a pure conscience, in the spirit of my fathers, when without ceasing I remember you night and day in my prayers . . .

2 TIMOTHY 1:3

Therefore I always exercise and discipline myself [mortifying my body, deadening my carnal affections, bodily appetites, and worldly desires, endeavoring in all respects] to have a clear (unshaken, blameless) conscience, void of offense toward God and toward men.

ACTS 24:16

A RESTORED CONSCIENCE

The restoration of true worship must come from the heart of the worshiper. It is not, and can never be, merely a learned behavior. God is interested in the heart of man above all else. If the heart is not pure, nothing that comes from the man is acceptable to God.

Paul spoke of the importance of keeping one's conscience clean. We cannot properly worship God with known sin in our lives. We must approach God with a clean conscience.

There is no peace for the person with a guilty conscience. His faith will not work; therefore, his prayers won't be answered. His excuses for sin will never stand in the presence of God.

One of the main functions of the Holy Spirit is to teach us all truth, to convict us of sin, and to convince us of righteousness (John 16:8, 13). Conviction is not meant to condemn; it is rather intended to provoke us to repentance. Through repentance and the power of forgiveness, our conscience is cleansed and purified. What good news! We can live before God with a perfectly clear conscience.

Let your conscience be your friend,
not a source of torment. Ask God to give you
a tender conscience toward Him.

DEALING WITH SHAME

You cannot get beyond your own opinion of
yourself—no matter how many good things
God may say about you in His Word.
Regardless of all the wonderful plans He
may have for your life, none of them will
come to pass without your cooperation.

GOD'S WORD FOR YOU

Therefore if any person is [ingrafted] in Christ (the Messiah) he is a new creation (a new creature altogether); the old [previous moral and spiritual condition] has passed away. Behold, the fresh and new has come! . . .

For our sake He made Christ [virtually] to be sin Who knew no sin, so that in and through Him we might become [endued with, viewed as being in, and examples of] the righteousness of God [what we ought to be, approved and acceptable and in right relationship with Him, by His goodness].

2 CORINTHIANS 5:17, 21

five
DEALING WITH SHAME

In my personal life, one area that I found to be very difficult to deal with was that of guilt and shame. I have previously addressed it in part, but I must expand upon it. In my many dealings with people, I have found the confusion surrounding this issue to be a huge problem to those who should be enjoying the power of forgiveness in their lives.

I carried a sense of guilt as long I could remember. Guilt was my constant companion. We went everywhere together! It began early in my childhood when I was being sexually abused. Even though my abuser told me that what he was doing was not wrong, it made me feel dirty and guilty. That only increased as I got older and became aware of just how wrong it was. I can never remember being guilt-free, even if I wasn't doing anything bad.

If you were told over and over as a youth that you were no good, there was something wrong with you, you couldn't do anything right, you were worthless and would never amount to anything, it is very possible you began to believe it and those thoughts took root in your life.

If your life was rooted in shame,
the power of forgiveness extends
to the deepest root.

GOD'S WORD FOR YOU

My dishonor is before me all day long, and shame has covered my face . . .

PSALM 44:15

ROOTED SHAME

There is a shame that is normal and healthy. If I lose or break something that belongs to someone else, I feel ashamed of my mistake. I am sorry, but I can ask forgiveness, receive it, and then go on with my life. Healthy shame reminds us that we are human beings with weaknesses and limitations.

In the Garden of Eden after the fall, Adam and Eve were ashamed when they realized they were naked (Genesis 3:6–8). They went and hid and tried to cover themselves. But that too was a normal reaction. If we sin, we feel bad about it until we repent and are forgiven.

But when an individual is rooted in shame, it poisons his entire life. He is not just ashamed of what he has done, he is ashamed of who he is. This person takes the shame into himself where it actually becomes the core of his being. Everything in his life becomes poisoned by his emotions so that he develops into a shame-based person.

The power of grace and forgiveness was sent to free us from the shame that would have us believe that something is wrong with us.

GOD'S WORD FOR YOU

For each tree is known and identified by its own fruit; for figs are not gathered from thornbushes, nor is a cluster of grapes picked from a bramblebush.

The upright (honorable, intrinsically good) man out of the good treasure [stored] in his heart produces what is upright (honorable and intrinsically good), and the evil man out of the evil storehouse brings forth that which is depraved (wicked and intrinsically evil); for out of the abundance (overflow) of the heart his mouth speaks.

LUKE 6:44–45

FRUIT OF SHAME

For the person who is rooted in shame, sooner or later the fruit will begin to manifest itself. Often in our fear of being seen for who we think we are, we try to be one way for one person or group and a totally different way for another. In our process of trying to avoid rejection by pleasing others, we lose track of who we really are and end up confused and miserable.

If we believe and feel that who we are is not acceptable, we may begin to hide our true feelings. Some people become so adept at repressing their true feelings they become emotionally frozen, unable to express any kind of feeling or emotion at all because it is too painful to do so. How many men put on a "macho" front and will not show any tenderness or sensitivity for fear they might appear weak or wimpish?

I found that I always felt defeated because no matter what I accomplished on the outside, I still felt bad about myself on the inside. I was ashamed of me! I didn't like who I was. I was continually rejecting my real self and trying to be someone or something I was not and never could be. That's the bad fruit of shame.

It's time to come out from behind our masks and become real. Only the Holy Spirit can teach us who we really are.

GOD'S WORD FOR YOU

May Christ through your faith [actually] dwell (settle down, abide, make His permanent home) in your hearts! May you be rooted deep in love and founded securely on love.

Ephesians 3:17

OUR "LOVE TANK"

Each one of us is born with a "love tank," and if our tank is empty, we are in trouble. We need to start receiving love from the moment we are born and continue receiving it—and giving it out—until the day we die.

Sometimes Satan manages to arrange things so that instead of receiving love, we receive hurts and abuse. If that arrangement continues, we become love-starved and warped, so that we are unable to maintain healthy relationships. If we can't get good feelings from within ourselves, we look for them on the outside. Many develop addictive behaviors of different types to try to find that inner satisfaction. They turn to sex, drugs, alcohol, tobacco, food, money, power, work, television, sports, and other addictive things to try to get some good feelings about themselves.

The good news is that whatever we may have been deprived of in the past, we can receive from the Lord. He is our Shepherd, so we shall not want (Psalm 23:1). He has promised not to withhold any good thing from us (Psalm 84:11). We can become rooted in His love and not rooted and grounded in the bad fruit tree of shame.

We don't have to go through another moment of our life with an empty "love tank." Receiving the love of God is the key.

GOD'S WORD FOR YOU

Blessed (happy, blithesome, joyous, spiritually prosperous—with life-joy and satisfaction in God's favor and salvation, regardless of their outward conditions) are the meek (the mild, patient, long-suffering), for they shall inherit the earth!

MATTHEW 5:5

TRUE MEEKNESS

A root of shame always manifests itself in abnormal ways. Bitterness, anger, and hostility produce pent-up emotions that don't get released properly. Some people actually think they deserve being taken advantage of and become doormats for everybody. They are mousy and wimpish.

I was not like that. I didn't even know who to be mad at. All I knew was that I was angry, and I was hurt. I was tired of being mistreated, and I wasn't going to take anything from anybody. I was always near what I call the "explode point." All it took was for someone to cross or offend me, or for something to go wrong, and I was ready to "blow up."

God wants to root our lives in the meekness of Jesus. We see in His life the power to repress and express anger at the right times. Meekness is the middle ground between emotional extremes. Meekness never allows anger to get out of control. It channels it in the right direction for the right purpose. We need to direct our anger away from people and ourselves and focus it on the source of our problem, the devil and his demons (Ephesians 6:12).

True meekness is getting angry at the right time in the right measure for the right reason.

GOD'S WORD FOR YOU

According as he hath chosen us in him before the foundation of the world, that we should be holy and without blame before him in love: . . .

To the praise of the glory of his grace, wherein he hath made us accepted in the beloved.

EPHESIANS 1:4, 6 KJV

Accepted in the Beloved

I remember standing in a prayer line where I overheard a woman next to me telling a pastor how she hated and despised herself. The pastor shocked her and me by stopping her and saying, "Who do you think you are? You have no right to hate yourself. God loved you so much that He sent His only Son to die for you . . . to suffer in your place. You have no right to hate or reject yourself. Your part is to receive what Jesus died to give you!"

Sometimes it takes a strong word to get us to see a trap that Satan has set for us. Self-rejection and self-hatred can almost sound pious to the shame-based person. They can become a way of punishing ourselves for our failures and inabilities.

God ordained us, destined us, planned in love for us to be adopted and accepted as His own children through His Son, Jesus Christ! Before we even existed, He chose us and set us apart to be blameless in His sight, above reproach before Him in love. With that knowledge, we should have our "love tanks" filled to overflowing!

Jesus bore your sins and shame and hatred and condemnation on the cross. What a glorious truth!

GOD'S WORD FOR YOU

For God so greatly loved and dearly prized the world that He [even] gave up His only begotten (unique) Son, so that whoever believes in (trusts in, clings to, relies on) Him shall not perish (come to destruction, be lost) but have eternal (everlasting) life.

JOHN 3:16

You shall love your neighbor as [you do] yourself.

MATTHEW 19:19

LOVING YOURSELF

I believe one of the greatest problems people have today concerns the way they feel about themselves. The truth is that most people carry around with them bad attitudes and negative self-images. Many of them have carried the negatives so long they don't even realize they have them.

What do you think of yourself? What kind of relationship do you have with yourself? No matter where you go or what you do in this life, you are always going to have to deal with you. There is no escaping from you.

The Lord commanded us to love ourselves as we love our neighbors. Many of us think we have worn God out with our failures and messes, but you can't do that. He loves us because He is Love. We need to love and accept ourselves as His creation. It begins when we are transplanted into His love and are rooted in Jesus. May He be your foundation and your root, so you will produce good fruit.

Receive God's love for you.
Bathe in it. Meditate on it.
Let it change and strengthen you.
Then give it away.

GOD'S WORD FOR YOU

Fear not, for you shall not be ashamed; neither be confounded and depressed, for you shall not be put to shame. For you shall forget the shame of your youth, and you shall not [seriously] remember the reproach of your widowhood any more.

ISAIAH 54:4

LIKING YOURSELF

It is not enough to love ourselves; we must also like ourselves. If you don't like yourself, you are going to have a hard time liking anyone else. If you're unhappy with yourself, you'll have trouble with others. You may pretend things are fine, but pretense doesn't alter the fact.

Because we are rooted and grounded in love, we can be relaxed and at ease, knowing that our acceptance is not based on our performance or perfect behavior. We can be secure in the knowledge that our value and worth are not dependent upon who we are or what we think or say or do. It is based on our relationship with Jesus.

To like ourselves simply means we accept ourselves as God's creation. We accept the fact that though we fail, that doesn't mean we are any less God's child.

Look at yourself in the mirror every morning and say, "I like you. You are a child of God. He loves you for who you are. You have gifts and talents. You are a neat person—and I like you." If you do that and really believe it, it will work wonders in overcoming a shame-based nature.

We need to be at peace with our past,
content with our present, and sure about our future,
knowing they are in God's loving hands.

GOD'S WORD FOR YOU

Instead of your [former] shame you shall have a twofold recompense; instead of dishonor and reproach [your people] shall rejoice in their portion. Therefore in their land they shall possess double [what they had forfeited]; everlasting joy shall be theirs.

ISAIAH 61:7

A TWOFOLD RECOMPENSE

If you are convinced that you have a shame-based nature or that you are rooted and grounded in shame, that curse can be broken off of you through the power of God. In Isaiah 54:4 and Isaiah 61:7, the Lord has promised to remove the shame and dishonor from us so that we remember it no more. He has promised that in their place He will pour out upon us a twofold blessing so that we possess double what we have lost, and that everlasting joy shall be ours.

Take your stand on the Word of God. Ask the Lord to work a healing miracle in your mind, will, and emotions. Let Him come in and fulfill what He came to do: heal your broken heart, bind up your wounds, give you beauty for ashes, joy for mourning, a garment of praise instead of heaviness, a double honor for a double shame.

Determine that from this moment on you are going to reject the roots of bitterness, shame, negativism, and perfectionism, and be rooted and grounded in the love of Christ.

Draw the bloodline of Jesus Christ across your life and boldly declare you are healed from the pains and wounds of your past and set free to live a new life of health and wholeness.

LIVING
FREE

*Refuse to live the rest of your life
in a prison of suspicion and fear! And
don't look to others to meet your needs.
Look to God. Anything people may do
to you, God can fix.*

GOD'S WORD FOR YOU

But Jesus [for His part] did not trust Himself to them, because He knew all [men];

And He did not need anyone to bear witness concerning man [needed no evidence from anyone about men], for He Himself knew what was in human nature. [He could read men's hearts.]

JOHN 2:24–25

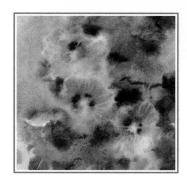

six

LIVING FREE

he power of forgiveness is the power of God to transform us from the inside out. Jesus is our example and role model for every aspect of our lives, and He demonstrated how we should live in relationship with other people.

Jesus did not trust people, because He knew human nature. He ate, drank, laughed, and wept with people. He confided in them and shared intimate things out of His heart with them. They were His friends, and He cared about them. But He did not trust Himself to them.

I think that means He did not become dependent upon them. He didn't throw Himself wide open to them. He didn't allow Himself to reach the place of feeling He could not get along without them. He purposely kept Himself in a position where He was primarily dependent upon God and God alone.

What the Lord is telling us is that He wants us to live our lives in balance. We must love our fellowman and maintain good fellowship with him. But we must never make the mistake of thinking we can trust others completely.

I cannot tell you, "Just trust people; they won't hurt you." We must face the reality that people hurt people.

GOD'S WORD FOR YOU

But far be it from me to glory [in anything or anyone] except in the cross of our Lord Jesus Christ (the Messiah), through Whom the world has been crucified to me, and I to the world!

GALATIANS 6:14

Thus says the Lord: Cursed [with great evil] is the strong man who trusts in and relies on frail man, making weak [human] flesh his arm, and whose mind and heart turn aside from the Lord.

JEREMIAH 17:5

Keeping a Proper Balance

The apostle Paul makes it clear he did not glory in anything or anyone, because the world was crucified to him and he to the world. What I think he meant was that he kept all things—including people, places, and positions—in proper balance in his life. He was not dependent upon anyone or anything for his joy and peace and victory in the Lord. He would not put pressure on relationships in an effort to get from people what only God could give him.

If we are not careful to maintain a proper balance in our lives, we will develop dependencies that Satan can play upon to destroy us and our effectiveness for Christ.

This is the balance God requires of us: When I look to myself to meet my needs, I fail; and when I look to others to meet my needs, they fail me. The Lord requires that He be allowed to meet our needs. When we look to Him, He often uses people to meet our needs, but we are looking to and depending on Him—not the people through whom He works.

Don't put pressure on other people
by expecting them to never disappoint,
fail, or hurt you.

GOD'S WORD FOR YOU

*And set your minds and keep them set on what is above
(the higher things), not on the things that are on the earth.
For [as far as this world is concerned] you have died,
and your [new, real] life is hidden with Christ in God.*

COLOSSIANS 3:2–3

ALIVE IN CHRIST

If you and I allow ourselves to become dependent on or addicted to things and people, the devil will use them to cause us all kinds of grief. That's why we must keep our eyes on Jesus and not on the things of this earth. As Paul was, you and I are "dead to this world" — and it is dead to us. We must not look to it for our help, but to the Lord.

You and I are never going to be whole and well mentally or emotionally or spiritually as long as we think we have to have some person or some thing. It might be nice to have them, but we don't have to have anybody or anything but God to get by!

Are you looking to people or things to make you happy? In my daily prayer sometimes I say, "Father, there is something I want, but I don't want to get out of balance or ahead of You. If it is Your will, I would like to have it. But if it is not Your will, then I can be happy without it because I want You to be number one in my life."

Trust God with the people in your life.
You may not be able to handle them,
but He is able.

GOD'S WORD FOR YOU

But be doers of the Word [obey the message], and not merely listeners to it, betraying yourselves [into deception by reasoning contrary to the Truth].

For if anyone only listens to the Word without obeying it and being a doer of it, he is like a man who looks carefully at his [own] natural face in a mirror;

For he thoughtfully observes himself, and then goes off and promptly forgets what he was like.

But he who looks carefully into the faultless law, the [law] of liberty, and is faithful to it and perseveres in looking into it, being not a heedless listener who forgets but an active doer [who obeys], he shall be blessed in his doing (his life of obedience).

JAMES 1:22–25

Doers of the Word

If you and I are to walk in the power and freedom of our forgiveness, we must become doers of the Word and not hearers only. Otherwise we are deceiving ourselves by going contrary to the truth.

It is the truth and the truth alone that will keep us set free. In order for that truth to work in our lives, we must be responsible. To receive what God promises us in His Word, we must obey the Word. We cannot try to excuse away our sins and weaknesses. Instead, we must become bond servants to God and not our human nature or to other people or things.

The bottom line is this: God is your Helper. He is your Healer. He has a personalized plan for your life in His Word. Make sure you know what it is, then begin to walk in obedience to the truth one step at a time. Obeying the Word requires consistency and diligence. It can't be hit and miss. We can't just try it to see if it works. There must be a dedication and commitment to do the Word whatever the outcome.

We will walk in victory if we do what the Lord says.

GOD'S WORD FOR YOU

Whoever will humble himself therefore and become like this little child [trusting, lowly, loving, forgiving] is greatest in the kingdom of heaven.

And whoever receives and accepts and welcomes one little child like this for My sake and in My name receives and accepts and welcomes Me.

MATTHEW 18:4–5

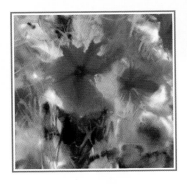

BECOME CHILDLIKE

You and I must humble ourselves and become as little children. While the Lord wants us to grow up in our attitude, behavior, and acceptance of responsibility in Christ (Ephesians 4:15), at the same time He wants us to be childlike in our dependence upon Him and in our free expression of our feelings toward Him.

One characteristic of a child is that he has fun no matter what he does. He manages to find a way to have a good time. God wants us to learn how to enjoy things and to enjoy Him. He wants us to enjoy prayer, Bible study, and going to church, just as He wants us to enjoy our spouse, children, family, home, and everything else in life, including the mundane. For too long we have put off enjoying life.

We need to find more humor in our everyday lives. And one of the first things we need to learn to laugh at is ourselves. Instead of getting all upset at our mistakes and shortcomings, we need to learn to laugh at our failures and foibles. As Art Linkletter used to say, "People are funny!" And that includes us.

Jesus wants us to walk in the freedom of little children.

GOD'S WORD FOR YOU

Now on the final and most important day of the Feast, Jesus stood, and He cried in a loud voice, If any man is thirsty, let him come to Me and drink!

He who believes in Me [who cleaves to and trusts in and relies on Me] as the Scripture has said, From his innermost being shall flow [continuously] springs and rivers of living water.

But He was speaking here of the Spirit, Whom those who believed (trusted, had faith) in Him were afterward to receive. For the [Holy] Spirit had not yet been given, because Jesus was not yet glorified (raised to honor).

JOHN 7:37–39

THE LIVING WATER

You and I are born with a nice, clean flowing well within us. Over time, Satan comes along and starts throwing stones into that well. By the time we are adults, our wells are so filled with stones that they have become stopped up. Every now and then we may feel a little gurgle down inside, but we never experience the water flowing freely.

Notice in John 7 that Jesus did not say that from those who believe in Him there will flow rivers of living water once in a while. He said these rivers of living water will flow continuously. That living water is the Holy Spirit. He quenches the deepest thirst of the soul.

That river of living water flows within all who have accepted Jesus as Lord and Savior. The Holy Spirit, that living water, empowers us to live according to God's will—a path that takes us to freedom.

Allowing the Holy Spirit to flow through you will not only water you but also those around you.

GOD'S WORD FOR YOU

Though the fig tree does not blossom and there is no fruit on the vines, [though] the product of the olive fails and the fields yield no food, though the flock is cut off from the fold and there are no cattle in the stalls,

Yet I will rejoice in the Lord; I will exult in the [victorious] God of my salvation!

The Lord God is my Strength, my personal bravery, and my invincible army; He makes my feet like hinds' feet and will make me to walk [not to stand still in terror, but to walk] and make [spiritual] progress upon my high places [of trouble, suffering, or responsibility]!

HABAKKUK 3:17–19

ℋANG TOUGH!

The Old Testament prophet Habakkuk spoke of hard times, calling them "high places," and stating that God had given him hinds' feet to scale those high places. A "hind" refers to a certain kind of deer that is an agile mountain climber. It can scale up what looks like a sheer cliff, leaping from ledge to ledge with great ease.

This is God's will for us, that when hardship comes our way we are not intimidated or frightened. To be truly victorious, we must grow to the place where we are not afraid of hard times but are actually challenged by them. In these verses these "high places" are referred to as "trouble, suffering, or responsibility." This is because it is during these times that we grow.

If you look back over your life, you will see that you never grow during easy times; you grow during hard times. During the easy times that come, you are able to enjoy what you have gained during the hard times. This is really a life principle; it is just the way it works.

God desires to restore you and me
to our rightful position of authority.
We were born destined for the throne,
not the ash heap of life.

GOD'S WORD FOR YOU

When you pass through the waters, I will be with you, and through the rivers, they will not overwhelm you. When you walk through the fire, you will not be burned or scorched, nor will the flame kindle upon you.

ISAIAH 43:2

Go All the Way Through

God wants us to be diligent and go all the way through with Him, not just go until the way becomes difficult, and then stop there. One of our greatest challenges is to face our mountains rather than trying to go around them.

Sometimes we go around and around the same mountain, and we end up like the Israelites in the wilderness who wandered around for forty years (Deuteronomy 2:1–3). We must learn to face our mountains and determine to go all the way through with God. That is the only path to victory.

I encourage you to go all the way through with God no matter how difficult it may seem. Let God have His way in your life. Pray for God's will and not your own will. God's way is for you to set your face like a flint, dig in both heels, and go all the way through.

Determine to enjoy the journey. Enjoying life is an attitude of the heart, a decision to enjoy everything because everything—even little, seemingly insignificant things—has a part in God's plan for our lives.

As we believe that it is God's will for us to experience continual joy, we will discover a power that lifts us above life's circumstances.

GOD'S WORD FOR YOU

And, [His completed experience] making Him perfectly [equipped], He became the Author and Source of eternal salvation to all those who give heed and obey Him . . .

HEBREWS 5:9

Looking away [from all that will distract] to Jesus, Who is the Leader and the Source of our faith [giving the first incentive for our belief] and is also its Finisher [bringing it to maturity and perfection]. He, for the joy [of obtaining the prize] that was set before Him, endured the cross, despising and ignoring the shame, and is now seated at the right hand of the throne of God.

HEBREWS 12:2

BRIDGES INSTEAD OF WALLS

Instead of the walls that I used to build around my life, I have learned to build bridges. By the power of grace and God's forgiveness, all the difficult and unfair things that have happened to me have been turned into highways over which others can pass to find the same liberty that I found.

God is no respecter of persons (Acts 10:34). What He has done for me, He will do for you, as long as His precepts are followed. You can discover the same freedom that I have found, and you can become a bridge for others to pass over, instead of a wall that shuts them out.

Jesus pioneered a pathway to God for us. He became a highway for us to pass over. He sacrificed Himself for us, and now that we are benefiting from His sacrifice, He is giving us a chance to sacrifice for others so they can reap the same benefits we enjoy. When my way gets hard, I remind myself that Jesus endured the cross for the joy of obtaining the prize that was set before Him.

Make a decision to tear down your walls and build bridges. There are many people who are lost in their messes and need someone to go before them and show them the way. Why not be that person for them?

A Celebration
of Simplicity

THE
SIMPLICITY
OF FAITH

To enjoy life to the full, keep it simple.

GOD'S WORD FOR YOU

Now while they were on their way, it occurred that Jesus entered a certain village, and a woman named Martha received and welcomed Him into her house.

And she had a sister named Mary, who seated herself at the Lord's feet and was listening to His teaching.

But Martha [overly occupied and too busy] was distracted with much serving; and she came up to Him and said, Lord, is it nothing to You that my sister has left me to serve alone? Tell her then to help me [to lend a hand and do her part along with me]!

But the Lord replied to her by saying, Martha, Martha, you are anxious and troubled about many things; there is need of only one or but a few things. Mary has chosen the good portion [that which is to her advantage], which shall not be taken away from her.

LUKE 10:38-42

one

THE SIMPLICITY OF FAITH

believe that life should be a celebration. Far too many believers don't even enjoy life, let alone celebrate it. Many people truly love Jesus Christ and are on their way to heaven, but very few are enjoying the trip. For many years I was one of those people . . . and so was Martha.

Martha was busy doing what I used to do, running around trying to make everything perfect in order to impress God and everyone else. I complicated my relationship with the Lord because I had a legalistic approach to righteousness. I pursued many things—answers to my situations, prosperity, healing, success in my ministry, changes in my family. I only felt good about myself when I was accomplishing something. And I resented people like Mary, who enjoyed themselves. I thought they should be doing what I was doing.

My problem was that I was all Martha and no Mary. I loved Jesus, but I had not learned about the simple life He desired me to live. The answer, I discovered, was rooted in faith, discovering what it means to sit at the feet of Jesus, listen to His words, and trust God with all of my heart and soul.

If you want to live a complicated, complex, joyless life, spend your time trying to do something that can't be done without God.

135

GOD'S WORD FOR YOU

But I fear, lest somehow, as the serpent deceived Eve by his craftiness, so your minds may be corrupted from the simplicity that is in Christ.

2 CORINTHIANS 11:3 NKJV

In [this] freedom Christ has made us free [and completely liberated us]; stand fast then, and do not be hampered and held ensnared and submit again to a yoke of slavery [which you have once put off].

GALATIANS 5:1

ONLY JESUS!

Jesus came to this world and paid for our sins, taking our punishment upon Himself. He became our substitute, paid the debt we owed, at no cost to us. He did all this freely because of His great love, grace, and mercy. He inherited all the Father has to give and tells us that we are joint-heirs with Him by virtue of our faith. He has provided the way for our complete victory both here and hereafter. We are more than conquerors. He has conquered, and we get the reward without the battle.

How much simpler could it be? The gospel is wonderfully uncomplicated.

Complication is the work of Satan. He hates simplicity because he knows the power and the joy that our faith brings. Whenever your relationship with God becomes complex, bewildering, and confusing, consider the source—doubt and unbelief are being mixed and twisted together with belief.

Return to and celebrate the simplicity of your faith in Jesus alone!

Believing is so much simpler
than not believing.

GOD'S WORD FOR YOU

And He called a little child to Himself and put him in
the midst of them and said, Truly I say to you, unless you
repent (change, turn about) and become like little children
[trusting, lowly, forgiving], you can never enter the
kingdom of heaven [at all].

Whoever will humble himself therefore and become
like this little child [trusting, lowly, loving, forgiving] is
greatest in the kingdom of heaven.

MATTHEW 18:2-4

So if the Son liberates you [makes you free men], then
you are really and unquestionably free.

JOHN 8:36

GLORIOUS FREEDOM

Children believe what they are told. Some people say children are gullible; meaning they believe anything no matter how ridiculous it sounds. But children are not gullible; they are trusting. It is a child's nature to trust unless he has experienced something that teaches him otherwise. And another thing we all know about children is that they can literally enjoy just about anything, even turning work into games.

Our heavenly Father desires us to come to Him as children. He wants us to know that we are His precious little ones and to put our complete faith in Him to care for us. He wants us to take His hand and lean on Him, continually asking for His help. Everything that God calls us to do, He must help us do. He is ready, waiting, and more than willing. But we must come humbly as little children—sincere, unpretentious, honest, open—knowing that without Him, we can do nothing.

As God's children we were never intended to live in bondage of any kind. We should be experiencing glorious freedom and liberty—freedom to enjoy all that God has given us in Christ. He has given us life, and our goal should be to enjoy it.

Seek to become and remain childlike with all the simplicity of a child. It will enhance the quality of your life in a most amazing way.

GOD'S WORD FOR YOU

Some trust in and boast of chariots and some of horses, but we will trust in and boast of the name of the Lord our God.

PSALM 20:7

Lean on, trust in, and be confident in the Lord with all your heart and mind and do not rely on your own insight or understanding.

PROVERBS 3:5

MARVELOUS DIVIDENDS

There are many facets of faith. The most brilliant facet, however, is trust! Trust is something we have, and we decide what to do with it. We decide in whom or in what to put our trust.

Where have you placed your trust? Is your trust in your job, employer, bank account, or friends? Perhaps your trust is in yourself, your past record of successes, education, natural talents, or possessions. All of these are temporal, subject to change. Only the Lord changes not. He alone is the Rock that cannot be moved.

As children of God, we must remember Who delivered us in the past and know Who will deliver us in current troubles, then take our trust and put it in the right place, which is in God alone. Trust is not upset, because it has entered into God's rest. Trust is not confused, because it has no need to lean to its own understanding. Trust does not indulge in carnal reasoning; it lets God be God.

Choose to place your trust in God. It requires a greater faith, but it pays marvelous dividends.

GOD'S WORD FOR YOU

Jesus replied, This is the work (service) that God asks of you: that you believe.

JOHN 6:29

Truly I tell you, whoever says to this mountain, Be lifted up and thrown into the sea! and does not doubt at all in his heart but believes that what he says will take place, it will be done for him.

For this reason I am telling you, whatever you ask for in prayer, believe (trust and be confident) that it is granted to you, and you will [get it].

MARK 11:23-24

142

*B*ELIEVE!

God's plan for us is actually so simple that many times we miss it. We tend to look for something more complicated—something more difficult—that we are expected to do to please God. Jesus has told us what we are to do to please the Father, "Believe!"

Doubt brings in confusion and often depression. It causes us to speak doubtful and negative words. Believing, on the other hand, releases joy and leaves us free to enjoy life while God is taking care of our circumstances. It sounds almost too good to be true, which is why many people never enter into God's plan.

When Jesus said that whatever we ask of God, believing, will be granted to us, He was saying that we will receive it *free*. In God's economy, everything comes to us as a gift, and the only thing we can do with a gift is receive it graciously with a thankful heart.

Faith is not the price that buys God's blessing. It is the hand that receives His blessing. The price was paid for us by Jesus Christ on the cross.

Faith, like muscle, is strengthened
by "using" it, not by talking about it.

GOD'S WORD FOR YOU

*For it is by free grace (God's unmerited favor)
that you are saved (delivered from judgment and made
partakers of Christ's salvation) through [your] faith.
And this [salvation] is not of yourselves [of your own
doing, it came not through your own striving], but it is
the gift of God;*

*Not because of works [not the fulfillment of the Law's
demands], lest any man should boast. [It is not the result
of what anyone can possibly do, so no one can pride
himself in it or take glory to himself.]*

EPHESIANS 2:8-9

*For we have heard of your faith in Christ Jesus [the
leaning of your entire human personality on Him in
absolute trust and confidence in His power, wisdom, and
goodness] and of the love which you [have and show] for
all the saints (God's consecrated ones).*

COLOSSIANS 1:4

FAITH AND GRACE

Over the past ten years I heard so much about faith that I was about to kill myself trying to believe God for all kinds of stuff without understanding the grace of God. I didn't know how to lean on God, how to rely on the Lord, how to totally trust my heavenly Father in every situation of life. The problem was that I was trusting my faith to meet my needs rather than trusting my God.

If everything is based on our faith alone, we will end up frustrated, trying to make things happen that we have no power to make happen. I was trying to believe God for healing and prosperity and a happy family life—and it wasn't working. So I tried to believe God more, which only led to more frustration, unhappiness, and discouragement.

The mistake I made was trying to make things happen by faith, by believing God. Instead, I had to learn to get beyond that to relying on the grace of God. When I did that, when I gave up all my works, then my frustration ceased. I realized that no matter how much faith I had, if God did not come through my faith by His grace to answer my needs, I was never going to receive anything.

The Holy Spirit works to get our eyes off our ability to believe and onto God's faithfulness and willingness to meet our need.

GOD'S WORD FOR YOU

. . . be vigilant and cautious at all times; for that enemy of yours, the devil, roams around like a lion roaring [in fierce hunger], seeking someone to seize upon and devour.

Withstand him; be firm in faith [against his onset— rooted, established, strong, immovable, and determined].

1 PETER 5:8-9

So be subject to God. Resist the devil [stand firm against him], and he will flee from you.

JAMES 4:7

THE PURPOSE OF FAITH

We must remember that the devil is not going to just sit back and allow us to take new ground without putting up a fight. Any time we begin to make progress in building the Kingdom of God, our enemy is going to come against us.

Many times the mistake we make is trying to use faith to get to the place where there is total freedom from trouble. The purpose of faith is not always to keep us from having trouble; it is often to carry us through trouble. If we never had any trouble, we wouldn't need any faith.

The temptation exists to run away from our problems, but the Lord says that we are to go through them. The good news is that He has promised that we will never have to go through them alone. He will always be there to help us in every way. He has said to us, "Fear not, for I am with you."

In our daily experience, we must learn to stand our ground and back the devil off our property, to drive him out of different areas of our lives. Learning to be stable in hard times is one of the best ways to do this.

The devil will give up when he sees that you are not going to give in.

GOD'S WORD FOR YOU

I have learned how to be content (satisfied to the point where I am not disturbed or disquieted) in whatever state I am.

PHILIPPIANS 4:11

FAITH AND CONTENTMENT

The Bible teaches us to be content no matter what our circumstances may be (Hebrews 13:5 KJV). We are not to be upset about anything, no matter what is happening. Instead, we are to pray about it and tell God our need. While we are waiting for Him to move, we are to be thankful for all that God has done for us already (Philippians 4:6).

I have discovered that the secret of being content is to ask God for what I want, knowing that if it is right, He will bring it to pass at the right time. And if it is not right, He will do something much better than what I asked for.

We must learn to trust God completely if we ever intend to enjoy peaceful living. We must meditate on what God has done in our life instead of what we are still waiting on Him to do.

God loves you. He is a good God Who only does good things. Be content knowing that His way is perfect, and He brings with Him a great recompense of reward for those who trust in Him (Hebrews 10:35 KJV).

Trust God. Hide yourself in Him.

❧

God is working in secret, behind the scenes even when it looks as though nothing will ever change.

GOD'S WORD FOR YOU

Therefore humble yourselves . . . casting the whole of your care [all your anxieties, all your worries, all your concerns, once and for all] on Him, for He cares for you affectionately and cares about you watchfully.

1 PETER 5:6-7

HE CARES FOR YOU

Worry, anxiety, and care have no positive effect on our lives. They do not bring a solution to problems. They do not help us achieve good health, and they prevent our growth in the Word of God.

One of the ways that Satan steals the Word of God from our heart is through cares. The Bible says we are to cast our cares onto God, which is done by prayer. We cannot handle our own problems; we are not built for it. We are created by God to be dependent upon Him, to bring Him our challenges, and to allow Him to help us with them.

We must not take the care upon ourselves. Keeping our cares is a manifestation of pride. It shows that we think we can solve our own problems and that we don't need the Lord.

We show our humility by leaning on God. Worry, anxiety, and care are not manifestations of leaning on God, but they clearly state by their mere existence that we are attempting to take care of ourselves.

Pray about everything and worry about nothing. You will enjoy life much more.

God's ability to bring His will to pass in your life is determined by your faith in Him and in His Word.

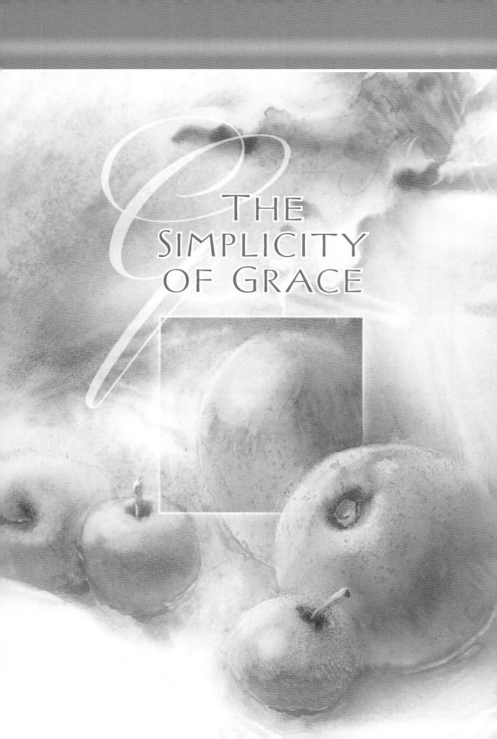

THE
SIMPLICITY
OF GRACE

Grace is God doing us a favor,
coming in with His power and might
to accomplish in and through us
what we don't deserve for Him to do.

GOD'S WORD FOR YOU

Let me ask you this one question: Did you receive the
[Holy] Spirit as the result of obeying the Law and doing its
works, or was it by hearing [the message of the Gospel]
and believing [it]? [Was it from observing a law of rituals
or from a message of faith?]

Are you so foolish and so senseless and so silly?
Having begun [your new life spiritually] with the [Holy]
Spirit, are you now reaching perfection [by dependence]
on the flesh?

Have you suffered so many things and experienced so
much all for nothing (to no purpose)—if it really is to no
purpose and in vain?

Then does He Who supplies you with His marvelous
[Holy] Spirit and works powerfully and miraculously
among you do so on [the grounds of your doing] what the
Law demands, or because of your believing in and
adhering to and trusting in and relying on the message that
you heard?

GALATIANS 3:2-5

two

THE SIMPLICITY
OF GRACE

here is nothing more powerful than the grace
of God. Everything in the Bible—salvation,
the infilling of the Holy Spirit, fellowship
with God, and all victory in our daily lives—is based
upon it. Without grace, we are nothing, we have
nothing, can do nothing. If it were not for the grace
of God, we would all be miserable and hopeless.

The grace of God is not complicated or confusing.
In fact, it is so simple that many of us miss its true
meaning and end up making our lives incredibly
complex. I know I did.

Reading God's Word, I constantly saw the need
for change in my life. But I didn't know that the grace
of God could bring about those changes. I didn't know
how to allow the Holy Spirit to come into my life and
cause the things to happen. So I tried to change
myself to be everything the Word said I was to be. I
also tried to change everything else in my life—my
husband, my children, and any circumstances I
thought were the cause of my problems. The results
went beyond frustration into becoming destructive.

I thank God that He did not leave me there.

*Grace is the power of God available to meet our needs
without any cost to us. It is received by believing rather
than through our own effort.*

GOD'S WORD FOR YOU

But He gives us more and more grace (power of the Holy Spirit, to meet this evil tendency and all others fully). . . . God sets Himself against the proud . . . but gives grace [continually] to the lowly (those who are humble enough to receive it).

JAMES 4:6

More and More Grace

All human beings have evil tendencies, but James teaches us that God will give us more and more grace to meet these tendencies.

I spent much of my Christian life trying to overcome my own wrong motives and intentions. All my trying brought much frustration. I had to come to a place of humility. I had to learn that God gives grace to the humble—not the proud.

We have our own ideas about what we can accomplish, but often we think more highly of ourselves than we ought. We should have a humble attitude, knowing that apart from God, we can do nothing.

If you are planning your own way, trying to make things happen in the strength of your own flesh, then you are frustrated. You probably have said, "No matter what I do, nothing seems to work!" Nothing will ever work until you learn to trust in God's grace.

Relax. Let God be God. Stop being so hard on yourself. Change is a process; it comes little by little. You're on your way to perfection, so enjoy the trip.

If you desire to be free, you must be willing to exchange trying for trusting. You must be willing to stop doing and start asking.

GOD'S WORD FOR YOU

But that no man is justified by the law in the sight of
God, it is evident: for, The just shall live by faith.

And the law is not faith: but, The man that doeth
them shall live in them.

Christ hath redeemed us from the curse of the law,
being made a curse for us: for it is written, Cursed is
every one that hangeth on a tree.

GALATIANS 3:11-13 KJV

[Therefore, I do not treat God's gracious gift as
something of minor importance and defeat its very
purpose]; I do not set aside and invalidate and frustrate
and nullify the grace (unmerited favor) of God. For if
justification (righteousness, acquittal from guilt) comes
through [observing the ritual of] the Law, then Christ (the
Messiah) died groundlessly and to no purpose and in vain.
[His death was then wholly superfluous.]

GALATIANS 2:21

GRACE VERSUS WORKS

It is curious that we come to God through Christ just as we are, relying on nothing but the blood of Jesus to cleanse us from our sins. Our hearts are full of gratitude because we know we don't deserve it. But from that moment on, for some reason we want to deserve everything else He gives us. From then on, God has to practically force every single blessing upon us because we think we don't deserve it. We didn't read the Bible enough, didn't pray enough, or lost our temper in traffic. We find a million ways to be disqualified from God's favor.

Despite all our emphasis on faith, we try to live by works a life that was brought into being and designed by God to be lived by grace. It's no wonder we feel frustrated and confused—both are signs that we are out of grace and into works.

When you have a problem in your life that you do not know how to handle, what you need is not more figuring and reasoning, but more grace. If you can't find a solution to your problem, then you need the Lord to reveal it to you.

The more you fret and strain over it, the more unlikely you are to see the solution to it.

Where works fail, grace always succeeds.
Do not frustrate the grace of God.

GOD'S WORD FOR YOU

So I asked the angel who talked with me, What are these, my lord?

Then the angel who talked with me answered me, Do you not know what these are? And I said, No, my lord.

Then he said to me, This [addition of the bowl to the candlestick, causing it to yield a ceaseless supply of oil from the olive trees] is the word of the Lord to Zerubbabel, saying, Not by might, nor by power, but by My Spirit [of Whom the oil is a symbol], says the Lord of hosts.

ZECHARIAH 4:4-6

Get Plugged In!

In our Christian walk, many times we end up with a lot of principles, formulas, and methods, but no real power. That may be true for teachings on faith, prayer, praise, meditation, Bible study, confession, spiritual warfare, and all the other precepts we have been hearing about and engaging in. They are all good, and we need to know about them, but alone they cannot solve our problems.

We must remember that, as good as all these disciplines are, they are only channels to receiving from the Lord. They are of no help unless they are plugged into the divine power source.

We get plugged in through a personal relationship with God, which requires time. We will never have any real lasting victory in our Christian life without spending time in personal, private fellowship with the Lord. He has an individual plan for you. If you ask Him, He will come into your heart and commune with you. He will teach and guide you in the way you should go.

Learn to respond quickly to the promptings of the Holy Spirit. Come apart with Him privately, and you will be rewarded in abundance.

*It is only in the presence of the Lord
that we receive the power of the Lord.*

GOD'S WORD FOR YOU

Now to a laborer, his wages are not counted as a favor or a gift, but as an obligation (something owed to him).

But to one who, not working [by the Law], trusts (believes fully) in Him Who justifies the ungodly, his faith is credited to him as righteousness (the standing acceptable to God).

ROMANS 4:4-5

Through Him also we have [our] access (entrance, introduction) by faith into this grace (state of God's favor) in which we [firmly and safely] stand. And let us rejoice and exult in our hope of experiencing and enjoying the glory of God.

ROMANS 5:2

GRACE IS NOT FOR SALE

The devil wants you and me to think that we can buy the grace of God. But God's grace is not for sale, because by its very definition—*unmerited* favor—it is a gift.

Grace cannot be bought by prayer, good works, Bible readings, or confessing Scriptures. It cannot even be bought by faith. The grace of God is receivable, but it is not "buyable."

We must be very careful that even when we operate by all the right methods our motives are pure. Even when we are fellowshipping with the Lord, if our motive is to get something from Him, we have moved from grace to works. Let us not fall into the trap of thinking that we *deserve* anything good from the Lord. Anytime we get wrapped up in self and ego we are on dangerous ground. We must get beyond ourselves and our works and efforts and keep our eyes focused on God and His grace toward us.

We are to seek the Lord and to fellowship with Him for no other reason than the fact that we love Him and want to be in His presence.

Determination and willpower can only take you so far. When the flesh fizzles out—and it will—the whole thing will collapse, and so will you.

GOD'S WORD FOR YOU

Now unto him that is able to do exceeding abundantly above all that we ask or think, according to the power that worketh in us, unto him be glory in the church by Christ Jesus throughout all ages, world without end. Amen.

EPHESIANS 3:20 KJV

But He said, What is impossible with men is possible with God.

LUKE 18:27

THE DIVINE ENABLER

Our God is able to do far above and beyond anything that we can ever dare to hope, ask, or even think. We need to pray, to do the asking, in faith, in trust. That opens the channel. But it is God Who does the work, not us.

If you are struggling with changes that need to be made in your own personality, this word is especially for you. You can't change yourself. But thanks be to God, He can! He knows what is wrong with you, and He's ready and able to bring about the changes that you need if you just ask.

You and I don't have a problem that is too big for the grace of God. If our problem gets bigger, God's grace gets bigger. If our problem multiplies, so that we go from one to two or three or more, the grace of God also multiplies so that we are able to handle them.

It doesn't take any more faith to believe God for the answer to three problems than for the answer to two problems or even one problem. Either we believe our God is big enough to handle whatever we face, or we do not.

We think we are supposed to be achievers, and we are. But the way we achieve is to believe. That frees us from worry and reasoning.

GOD'S WORD FOR YOU

Let us then fearlessly and confidently and boldly draw near to the throne of grace (the throne of God's unmerited favor to us sinners), that we may receive mercy [for our failures] and find grace to help in good time for every need [appropriate help and well-timed help, coming just when we need it].

HEBREWS 4:16

Mountains of Grace

Our God is always with us. But sometimes mountains rise in front of us that seem bigger than He is. The temptation is to avoid the obstacles, to run away from the things that oppose us. In reality, we are running from the enemy, because he is the one who throws up the obstacles for that very purpose. I encourage you to face the enemy, to not be afraid or intimidated by what he throws at you.

One of the aspects that we fail to understand about God's grace is that although He has endless mountains of it, we must come to His throne constantly for assurance about today, peace about yesterday, and confidence about tomorrow. Though God is always leading us into situations that are over our head, He knows exactly what He's going to do. He has a plan, a path, and a work all ready for us.

No matter what happens, God is still in control. His grace is power, and it is sufficient to meet all our needs. Even through the most difficult of times, times of extraordinary pressure and stress, His divine, wonder-working power is equal to all life's challengers. Call on the Lord and He will provide.

God never leads us where He cannot keep us. His grace is always sufficient for us — in any and every circumstance of life.

GOD'S WORD FOR YOU

God selected (deliberately chose) what in the world is foolish to put the wise to shame, and what the world calls weak to put the strong to shame.

And God also selected (deliberately chose) what in the world is low-born and insignificant and branded and treated with contempt, even the things that are nothing, that He might depose and bring to nothing the things that are.

So that no mortal man should [have pretense for glorying and] boast in the presence of God.

1 CORINTHIANS 1:27-29

GRACE TO BE HIS AMBASSADORS

One time while I was reading about Smith Wigglesworth and his great faith, I was deeply impressed by all the wonderful things he did in his ministry. I thought, *Lord, I know I'm called, but I could never do anything like that.* Just that quickly, I sensed the Lord speak to my heart, "Why not? Aren't you as big a mess as anybody else?"

You see, we have it backward. We think God is looking for people who "have it all together." But that is not true. The Word of God says that God in His grace and favor chooses the weak and foolish things of the world in order to confound the wise. He is looking for those who will humble themselves and allow Him to work His will through them.

If you will be careful not to get haughty or arrogant, the Lord can use you just as mightily as any of the other great men and women of God. He doesn't choose us because we are able, but simply because we are available. That too is part of God's grace and favor that He pours out upon us when He chooses us as Christ's personal ambassadors.

You have as much right to God's favor as anyone else. Learn to avail yourself of it and walk in it.

GOD'S WORD FOR YOU

And I will pour out upon the house of David and upon the inhabitants of Jerusalem the Spirit of grace or unmerited favor and supplication.

ZECHARIAH 12:10

Now the Lord is the Spirit, and where the Spirit of the Lord is, there is liberty (emancipation from bondage, freedom).

And all of us, as with unveiled face, [because we] continued to behold [in the Word of God] as in a mirror the glory of the Lord, are constantly being transfigured into His very own image in ever increasing splendor and from one degree of glory to another; [for this comes] from the Lord [Who is] the Spirit.

2 CORINTHIANS 3:17-18

THE SPIRIT OF GRACE

One of the twenty-five biblical names used to refer to the Holy Spirit is the Spirit of grace and supplication. There is no way to live in victory without understanding the Holy Spirit's role in empowering our lives and in teaching us to pray, asking God for what we need rather than trying to make it happen on our own.

The Spirit of grace is the One Who brings every good gift into our life, everything we need. His multiple role as Comforter, Counselor, Helper, Intercessor, Advocate, Strengthener, and Standby can be summarized by saying that His purpose is to get right in the middle of our lives and make them all work out for the glory of God.

God is interested in every detail of your life. He wants to help with everything in your life. He stands by us at all times waiting for the first available opportunity to jump in and give us the help and strength we need. Learn one of the most spiritual prayers you can offer: "Help!" We have not because we ask not. Ask and ask and ask. Keep on asking so that you may receive and your joy may be full.

The grace of God doesn't just fall upon us; we must choose it. God's part is to give us His grace and Spirit; our part is to give Him our mind and will.

THE SIMPLICITY OF JOY AND PEACE

This is God's will for us, that we might have and enjoy life. Jesus did not die for you and me that we might be miserable. He died to deliver us from every kind of oppression and misery.

GOD'S WORD FOR YOU

*For the kingdom of God is not meat and drink; but
righteousness, and peace, and joy in the Holy Ghost.*

ROMANS 14:17 KJV

*May the God of your hope so fill you with all joy and
peace in believing [through the experience of your faith]
that by the power of the Holy Spirit you may abound and
be overflowing (bubbling over) with hope.*

ROMANS 15:13

three

THE SIMPLICITY OF JOY AND PEACE

It should never be this complicated, I thought, feeling miserable. Something was lurking inside, constantly draining the joy out of me. It began to dawn on me that I was doubting instead of believing. I was doubting the call of God on my life, wondering if He would meet our financial needs, questioning my decisions and actions.

I had become negative instead of positive. I was doubting instead of believing.

Doubt complicates everything. It creeps in through the door of your heart, filling your mind with reasoning that leads to negativity. It rotates around and around the circumstances or situations of your life, attempting to find answers for them.

The Word of God does not instruct us to search for our own answers. We are, however, instructed to trust God with all of our heart and soul (Proverbs 3:5). When we follow the simple guidelines the Lord has laid out for us, they will unerringly bring us to joy and peace.

When doubt knocks at your door, answer with a believing heart, and you'll always maintain the victory. That's a grand reason to celebrate.

Joy is never released through unbelief but is always present where there is belief.

175

GOD'S WORD FOR YOU

For the kingdom of God is not meat and drink; but righteousness, and peace, and joy in the Holy Ghost.

ROMANS 14:17 KJV

Joy

My understanding of *joy* is that it covers a wide range of emotions, from calm delight to extreme hilarity. The hilarious times are fun, and we all need those moments of laughing until our sides hurt. We probably won't live our daily lives that way, but we need those times. Why else would God give us the ability to laugh?

As Christians, we should grow in our ability to enjoy life and be able to say, "I live my life in a state of calm delight." I think calm delight is a mixture of peace and joy.

Some of the Greek words relating to joy in the Bible mean *delight, gladness, exceeding joyful, exuberant joy, to exult, rejoice greatly . . . with exceeding joy.* Webster defines it as *great pleasure or happiness, a source of pleasure or satisfaction, to fill with joy, or to enjoy.*

Whichever definition you prefer, the sad reality is that so few believers know the joy of the Lord. Don't let another day pass by without experiencing the Kingdom of God at its center—righteousness, peace, and joy in the Holy Spirit.

There is nothing as tragic
as being alive and not enjoying life.

GOD'S WORD FOR YOU

*The thief comes only to steal and kill and destroy; I
have come that they may have life, and have it to the full.*

JOHN 10:10 NIV

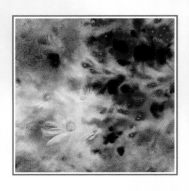

CELEBRATE LIFE

It is possible to live our lives blandly going through the motions of working, accomplishing, doing, but to never truly enjoy life. This is true of unbelievers, as well as believers, who have not learned to really enjoy the life God has given them. Jesus gave us life so we can derive pleasure from being alive, not just so we can go through the motions and try to survive until He comes back for us or takes us home.

Enjoying life is a decision that is not based on enjoyable circumstances. It is an attitude of the heart, a decision to enjoy everything because everything— even little, seemingly insignificant things—has a part in God's overall "big picture."

Doubt and unbelief are thieves of joy, but simple childlike believing releases the joy that is resident in our spirit because the Holy Spirit lives there. As we believe that it is God's will for us to experience continual joy, we will discover a power that lifts us above our life circumstances. We will be free to leave our problems in God's hands while we enjoy His blessings.

*We need to learn how to celebrate
in God's joy, to live life "to the full."*

GOD'S WORD FOR YOU

I do not consider, brethren, that I have captured and made it my own [yet]; but one thing I do [it is my one aspiration]: forgetting what lies behind and straining forward to what lies ahead,

I press on toward the goal to win the [supreme and heavenly] prize to which God in Christ Jesus is calling us upward.

PHILIPPIANS 3:13-14

Joy's Enemy #1

Regret of the past is a primary thief of joy and peace. Many people stay trapped in the past. Whether a mistake was made twenty years ago or ten minutes ago, there is nothing you can do about it except ask God's forgiveness, receive it, forget the past, and go on. There may be some restitution you can make to the person you hurt, and by all means do so. But the bottom line is that you still must let go of the past in order to grasp the future.

Like Paul, we are all pressing toward the mark of perfection, but none of us have arrived. I believe Paul thoroughly enjoyed his life journey and ministry, and this "one aspiration" of his was part of the reason why. He had learned to forget his mistakes and refused to live in regret of the past.

Always remember that regret steals *now*! God has called us to a faith walk in the *now*. When I cling to the past, I lay aside my faith and stop believing, then lose my peace and joy.

Let this be a day of decision for you—a day when you decide to no longer operate in regret. Become a now person. Live in the present. God has a plan for you now. Trust Him today.

God gives grace and joy and peace for today, but He does not give grace today for yesterday or tomorrow. Live life one day at a time.

GOD'S WORD FOR YOU

God did not give us a spirit of timidity (of cowardice, of craven and cringing and fawning fear), but [He has given us a spirit] of power and of love and of calm and well-balanced mind and discipline and self-control.

2 TIMOTHY 1:7

Then I said to you, Dread not, neither be afraid of them. The Lord your God Who goes before you, He will fight for you just as He did for you in Egypt before your eyes.

DEUTERONOMY 1:29-30

Joy's Enemy #2

Do you look forward to every day with a spirit of joy and peace of good things to come, or do you await each morning in a state of dread? Dread, whether of going to work or facing a life-threatening illness, is a subtle form of fear that the devil uses to steal our joy and prevent us from enjoying life. It prevents us from walking in the will of God and moving forward in the plans of God to receive the blessings of God.

Dread comes after us aggressively and violently and cannot be defeated passively. Letting negative feelings and thoughts come on you will destroy all your joy and peace. We must use our faith to aggressively defeat it. We must believe that Jesus goes before us and makes a way for us. When a project seems impossible or unpleasant, trust Him to make the way clear for you.

As Christians, we can do unpleasant things and enjoy them because the Holy Spirit is in us. We can enjoy Him in the midst of adverse and unpleasant conditions. Our joy comes from Who is *inside* us, not what is around us.

*If we set our minds to it, we can
enjoy everything we do in life.
Where God guides, He provides.*

GOD'S WORD FOR YOU

And the harvest of righteousness (of conformity to God's will in thought and deed) is [the fruit of the seed] sown in peace by those who work for and make peace [in themselves and in others, that peace which means concord, agreement, and harmony between individuals, with undisturbedness, in a peaceful mind free from fears and agitating passions and moral conflicts].

JAMES 3:18

Be well balanced (temperate, sober of mind), be vigilant and cautious at all times; for that enemy of yours, the devil, roams around like a lion roaring (in fierce hunger], seeking someone to seize upon and devour.

1 PETER 5:8

THE POWER OF JOY AND PEACE

If you have a problem and the devil cannot drive you to be upset about it, he has no power over you. Your power is in maintaining a calm, peaceful, trusting attitude. The devil's power is in causing you to be upset and fearful, thus depleting your strength.

When you find yourself in a troublesome situation, let your goal be to simply stay calm. Each time you begin to feel upset or frustrated, stop and ask yourself, "What is the enemy trying to do here?"

The Holy Spirit works in an atmosphere of joy and peace. He does not work in turmoil. In a time of trial, your strength is found in taking your position in Christ and entering into God's rest. All of these biblical words—*abide, still, rest, stand,* and *in Christ*— say the same basic thing: *Do not lose your joy and peace!*

We are not overcamers, but we are always to be overcomers. You will never have overcome every obstacle, but you can have the assurance of always triumphing in Christ. If you take each problem as it comes, it will work out all right. Jesus is always with you in each situation. Just remember to trust Him for enough joy and peace for today.

❦

If the devil can control you with circumstances, he will have you under his thumb all the time. You can walk in your authority by always being in peace.

GOD'S WORD FOR YOU

You will show me the path of life; in Your presence is fullness of joy, at Your right hand there are pleasures forevermore.

PSALM 16:11

ᶠULLNESS OF JOY

There are many wonderful benefits from simply spending time with God. The presence of the Lord is always with us, but we do not always recognize it or take time to be conscious of it.

There seems to be a great lack of joy and peace in the world but also among God's people. Many people spend their lives chasing things, when nothing can keep us satisfied except God Himself.

When people are not satisfied inwardly, they usually look for some outward object to satisfy their hunger. Often they end up in a fruitless search for that which cannot fill the emptiness within. We've heard it said, many people spend their lives climbing the ladder of success, only to find when they reach the top, their ladder is leaning against the wrong building.

When we keep our priorities straight, we discover that everything we really need in life is found in the Lord. Seek to dwell in His presence. In Him is the path of life, the fullness of joy, and pleasures forevermore.

*The reason we can laugh and enjoy life
in spite of our current circumstances
is because Jesus is our joy.*

GOD'S WORD FOR YOU

[After all] the kingdom of God is not a matter of [getting the] food and drink [one likes], but instead it is righteousness (that state which makes a person acceptable to God) and [heart] peace and joy in the Holy Spirit.

ROMANS 14:17

KINGDOM LIVING

God's Kingdom is not made up of worldly possessions but consists of something far greater and more beneficial. God does bless us with material possessions, but the Kingdom is much more than that: It is righteousness, peace, and joy in the Holy Spirit.

Righteousness is not the result of what we do, but rather what Jesus has done for us (1 Corinthians 1:30). When we accept this truth by faith and receive it personally, a great burden is lifted from us.

Peace is so wonderful—it is definitely Kingdom living. We are to pursue peace, crave it, and go after it (Psalm 34:14; 1 Peter 3:11). Jesus is our peace (Ephesians 2:14). God's will for you and me is peace beyond understanding (Philippians 4:7).

Joy can be anything from calm delight to extreme hilarity. Joy improves our countenance, our health, and the quality of our lives. It strengthens our witness to others and makes some of the less desirable circumstances of our life more bearable.

It is clear in the Word of God: Seek God and His Kingdom, and He will take care of everything else (Matthew 6:33).

God will bring to pass what you are believing for according to His will no matter how long it takes. This is one of the things that will keep you flowing with joy in His Kingdom.

GOD'S WORD FOR YOU

Be careful for nothing; but in every thing by prayer and supplication with thanksgiving let your requests be made known unto God.

And the peace of God, which passeth all understanding, shall keep your hearts and minds through Christ Jesus.

PHILIPPIANS 4:6-7 KJV

Casting the whole of your care [all your anxieties, all your worries, all your concerns, once and for all] on Him, for He cares for you affectionately and cares about you watchfully.

1 PETER 5:7

PRAYER AND PEACE

The peace that passes understanding is a great thing to experience. When, according to all the circumstances, you should be upset, in a panic, in turmoil, and worried yet you have peace, that is unexplainable. The world is starving for this kind of peace. You cannot buy it; it is not for sale. It is a free gift from Jesus, and it leads to joy unspeakable and full of glory.

The prayer of commitment is a powerful prayer that moves your burden from you onto Jesus. To *cast* means to pitch or throw vehemently. The sooner you do this the better. You do it through prayer. Commit your problems to His loving care. Do this as soon as the Holy Spirit makes you aware that you have lost your peace and joy. The longer you wait to resist, the stronger the devil's hold on you will become. Then it is harder to break free.

Jesus wants us to know that we are right with God because of what He has already done for us. He wants us to have incredible peace and joy in the midst of tribulation. Only He can give us that.

The believer who is experiencing God's peace through his relationship with Jesus can have peace even in the midst of the storms of life.

THE SIMPLICITY OF LOVE

What we need more than anything else is a revelation of God's love for us personally. This is the foundation for the victorious Christian life.

GOD'S WORD FOR YOU

And we know (understand, recognize, are conscious of, by observation and by experience), and believe (adhere to and put faith in and rely on) the love God cherishes for us. God is love, and he who dwells and continues in love dwells and continues in God, and God dwells and continues in him.

In this [union and communion with Him] love is brought to completion and attains perfection with us, that we may have confidence for the day of judgment [with assurance and boldness to face Him], because as He is, so are we in this world.

There is no fear in love [dread does not exist], but full-grown (complete, perfect) love turns fear out of doors and expels every trace of terror! For fear brings with it the thought of punishment, and [so] he who is afraid has not reached the full maturity of love [is not yet grown into love's complete perfection].

We love Him, because He first loved us.

1 JOHN 4:16-19

four
THE SIMPLICITY
OF LOVE

*L*oving and being loved are what make life worth living. To love is the way God created us, the energy of life. It gives life purpose and meaning. Love is the greatest thing in the world.

It is also the most fiercely attacked area in our lives. The devil's goal is to separate us from God's love, and he will use anything he can to complicate our understanding of God's love or make it confusing. His primary means of deception is to get us to believe that God's love for us depends on our worthiness.

Here's how it worked in my life. Whenever I failed, I would stop allowing myself to receive God's love and start punishing myself by feeling condemned and guilty. I lived this way for the first forty years of my life, faithfully carrying my heavy sack of guilt on my back everywhere I went. I made mistakes regularly, and I felt guilty about each one. Then I would try to win God's favor with good works.

The day of liberation finally came for me. God graciously revealed to me, through the Holy Spirit, His love for me personally. That single revelation changed my entire life and walk with Him.

God's love for you is perfect and unconditional.
When you fail, He keeps on loving you because
His love is not based on you but on Him.

195

GOD'S WORD FOR YOU

For God so greatly loved and dearly prized the world that He [even] gave up His only begotten (unique) Son, so that whoever believes in (trusts in, clings to, relies on) Him shall not perish (come to destruction, be lost) but have eternal (everlasting) life.

JOHN 3:16

And we know (understand, recognize, are conscious of, by observation and by experience) and believe (adhere to and put faith in and rely on) the love God cherishes for us. God is love, and he who dwells and continues in love dwells and continues in God, and God dwells and continues in him.

1 JOHN 4:16

GREATLY LOVED

Many of us believe that God loves the world, but we're not as certain about His love for us specifically. Some of us feel He loves us as long as we don't mess up. We concluded long ago that God can't be very impressed with us.

We have it all wrong. God loves us. God loves *you*! You are special to Him. He doesn't love you because you are a good person or do everything right. He loves you because He is love. Love is not something God does; it is Who He is.

God's love cannot be earned or deserved. It must be received by faith. His love is pure and ever flowing. He is everlasting God, and you can't wear Him out. Many of us think we have worn God out with our failures and messes, but you cannot do that. He may not always love everything you do, but He does love you. Love is His unfailing nature.

No matter how hard you seek the things of God, if you have not received the fact that God loves you, you are not going to get far.

Let God love you. Receive His love for you. Bathe in it. Meditate on it. Let it change and strengthen you. Then give it away.

If you had been the only person on the face of this earth, Jesus would have gone through all the suffering for you. His love for you is everlasting.

GOD'S WORD FOR YOU

*To appoint unto them that mourn in Zion, to give
unto them beauty for ashes.*

ISAIAH 61:3 KJV

*For I will restore health to you, and I will heal your
wounds, says the Lord, because they have called you an
outcast, saying, This is Zion, whom no one seeks after
and for whom no one cares!*

JEREMIAH 30:17

BEAUTY FOR ASHES

Everyone experiences some rejection in this life, and the memories and scars can be deep. Thousands of people have been hurt severely. They come from broken relationships or abusive backgrounds that are still producing bad fruit in their personalities.

The Lord has consistently taught me that bad fruit comes from a bad root. No matter how much we may try to get rid of the bad fruit, unless the root is dealt with, more bad fruit will crop up.

Some of us need to be transplanted into God's love. If we started in the wrong soil, He will transplant us so that we can get rooted and grounded in Jesus. He created us to be loved. He wants to love us; He wants us to love one another, and He wants us to love and accept ourselves. Without this root, there will be no joy and peace.

God wants to send the wind of the Holy Spirit into our lives (Acts 2:1-4) to blow away the ashes that are left behind from Satan's attempt to destroy us and to replace those ashes with beauty.

Know that you are valuable, unique, loved, and special. With this as your foundation and your root, you will produce good fruit.

God desires to heal you from past hurts caused by rejection. He wants you to know He will never reject you because of your weaknesses.

GOD'S WORD FOR YOU

If I [can] speak in the tongues of men and [even] of angels, but have not love (that reasoning, intentional, spiritual devotion such as is inspired by God's love for and in us), I am only a noisy gong or a clanging cymbal.

And if I have prophetic powers (the gift of interpreting the divine will and purpose), and understand all the secret truths and mysteries and possess all knowledge, and if I have [sufficient] faith so that I can remove mountains, but have not love (God's love in me) I am nothing (a useless nobody).

Even if I dole out all that I have [to the poor in providing] food, and if I surrender my body to be burned or in order that I may glory, but have not love (God's love in me), I gain nothing.

1 CORINTHIANS 13:1-3

THE GREATEST OF THESE IS LOVE

This is strong language, but hopefully it will wake us up!

There are many people who think they are really something because of what they have accomplished in life, but according to God's Word, they are nothing unless love has been a priority in their life.

Of course, the way Jesus sees how much we love Him is by how much we obey Him. He has commanded us to love one another; if we are not doing that, then we are not showing Him that we love Him.

We can sacrifice without love, we can give without proper motive, we can build ministries and forget all about love, but there is nothing greater we can take to the unchurched world than love. There is nothing more convincing than God's love reflected in our own character.

Love is the universal language; everyone understands it. Love can melt the hardest heart, it can heal the wounds of the broken heart, and it can quiet the fears of the anxious heart.

Love should be number one on our spiritual priority list. We should study love, pray about love, and develop the fruit of love by practicing loving others.

GOD'S WORD FOR YOU

In this is love: not that we loved God, but that He loved us and sent His Son to be the propitiation (the atoning sacrifice) for our sins.

Beloved, if God loves us so [very much], we also ought to love one another.

1 JOHN 4:10-11

Give Away God's Love

Having God's love in us, we can give it away. We can choose to love others lavishly. We can love them unconditionally as He has loved us.

Everyone in the world desires to be loved, to be accepted. The love of God is the most wonderful gift we are given. It flows to us, and then it should flow through us out to others.

For much of our lives, we try to find happiness the wrong way. We attempt to find it in getting, but it is found in giving.

Love must give; it is the nature of love to do so: "For God so greatly loved and dearly prized the world that He [even] gave up His only begotten (unique) Son, so that whoever believes in (trusts in, clings to, relies on) Him shall not perish (come to destruction, be lost) but have eternal (everlasting) life" (John 3:16).

We show love to others by meeting their needs—practical needs as well as spiritual needs. Generosity is love in action.

God wants to pour out His love
into our lives so that we can pour it out
to a hurting world.

GOD'S WORD FOR YOU

Love endures long and is patient.

1 CORINTHIANS 13:4

Love Is Patient

Love is seen as we are patient with one another.

The world today is filled with impatient people. It seems that everyone is in a hurry. Stress levels are very high in the lives of most people, and the pressure they live under provokes impatience. Even Christians are as prone to impatience as everybody else.

Love is patient. It is not in a hurry. It always takes time to wait on God, to fellowship with Him.

A person whose life is marked by love is patient with people. He is even patient with himself, with his own frailties and weaknesses. He is also kind. He takes the time to listen to the elderly person who is lonely and wants to talk. He is willing to listen to the same story four or five times just to show kindness.

Patience is a wonderful virtue. It is one facet of love that must be developed by the person who is seeking to have a strong love walk and display the character of Jesus Christ.

Learn to respond patiently in all kinds of trials, and you will find yourself living a quality of life that is not just endured but enjoyed to the full.

GOD'S WORD FOR YOU

. . . it is not touchy or fretful or resentful; it takes no account of the evil done to it [it pays no attention to a suffered wrong].

1 CORINTHIANS 13:5

. . . forgiving one another [readily and freely], as God in Christ forgave you.

EPHESIANS 4:32

ℒOVE DOES NOT HOLD GRUDGES

Love forgives; it does not hold a grudge. It is not touchy, easily offended, nor is it fretful or resentful. Some people get their feelings hurt about everything. It is very difficult to be in a relationship with people like this.

We have many opportunities every day to get offended; each time we must make a choice. If we choose to live by our feelings, we will never flow in this all-important facet of love.

"Drop it, leave it and let it go," is what the Bible says we are to do with offenses (Mark 11:25). It is important to forgive quickly. The quicker we do it, the easier it becomes. A weed that has deep roots is harder to pull out than one that has just sprung up.

God is love, and He forgives and forgets: "For I will forgive their iniquity, and their sin I will remember no more" (Jeremiah 31:34). And He is glad to do so. If we want to be like Him, then we must develop the same habit.

If we are to walk the narrow path,
Jesus says that we will have to learn
to be quick to forgive.

GOD'S WORD FOR YOU

The Spirit of the Lord God is upon me, because the Lord has anointed and qualified me to preach the Gospel of good tidings to the meek, the poor, and afflicted; He has sent me to bind up and heal the brokenhearted, to proclaim liberty to the [physical and spiritual] captives.

ISAIAH 61:1

Now the Lord is the Spirit, and where the Spirit of the Lord is, there is liberty (emancipation from bondage, freedom). [Isa. 61:1, 2.]

2 CORINTHIANS 3:17

Love Is Liberating

Love offers people both roots and wings. It provides a sense of belonging (roots) and a sense of freedom (wings). Love does not try to control or manipulate others. It does not try to reach fulfillment through the destiny of others.

Jesus said that He was sent by God to proclaim liberty. As believers, that is what we are meant to do also—to free people to fulfill God's will for their lives, not to bring them under our control.

How many parents push their children to do things they do not even want to do just to meet the frustrated desires of the parents?

That is not the way true love works. It does not try to gain personal satisfaction at the expense of others.

If you and I really love something, we must take a chance on setting it free. If it really belongs to us, it will come back to us.

A caged bird cannot fly!

Proclaim liberty. Set people free and see what they do.

❧

*God wants us to release the people in our life
to be all they can be for His glory, not our own.*

GOD'S WORD FOR YOU

Render to all men their dues. [Pay] taxes to whom taxes are due, revenue to whom revenue is due, respect to whom respect is due, and honor to whom honor is due.

ROMANS 13:7

Love Shows Respect

Love respects the differences in other people. A selfish person expects everyone to be just the way he is and to like whatever he likes.

Respecting individual rights is very important. If God had wanted us to all be alike, He would not have given each of us a different set of fingerprints. I think that one fact alone proves that we are created equal, but different.

We all have different gifts and talents, different likes and dislikes, different goals in life, different motivations, and the list goes on and on.

Love shows respect; the person who loves has learned to give freedom to those he loves. Freedom is one of the greatest gifts we can give. It was what Jesus came to give us, and we must also give it to others.

All of God's creation has great worth and should be treated as such. Since people are the height of His creation, they should be treated with great respect and considered very valuable.

Unconditional love unselfishly loves selfish people, generously gives to stingy people, and continually blesses unappreciative people.

GOD'S WORD FOR YOU

. . . love never is envious nor boils over with jealousy.

1 CORINTHIANS 13:4

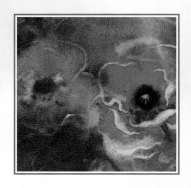

*L*OVE IS NOT ENVIOUS OR JEALOUS

According to Proverbs 14:30, ". . . envy, jealousy, and wrath are like rottenness of the bones."

In the Word of God, we are commanded not to covet anything that belongs to another person (Exodus 20:17). We are not to be envious or jealous because these sins poison our own life and hinder loving relationships with others.

I have discovered the best way to get over envy or jealously is to admit it. When you begin to feel jealous or envious, be honest with God and ask Him to help you live free from it.

I must admit, there are times when I hear about a blessing that someone has received, and I start to think, *When is that going to happen to me?* When that thought enters my mind, I immediately open my mouth and say, "I am happy for him. If God can do it for him, He can do it for me too."

We should bless others and not be afraid they will get ahead of us. We must not envy anyone else's appearance, possessions, education, social standing, marital status, gifts and talents, job, or anything else because it will only hinder our own blessing.

We all have gifts that God has given us;
they don't come from any other source.

THE SIMPLICITY OF FORGIVENESS

Forgiveness is a gift given to those who do not and will never deserve it. Being forgiven is as simple as freely receiving a gift and is never more complicated than that.

GOD'S WORD FOR YOU

In Him we have redemption (deliverance and salvation) through His blood, the remission (forgiveness) of our offenses (shortcomings and trespasses), in accordance with the riches and the generosity of His gracious favor.

EPHESIANS 1:7

If we [freely] admit that we have sinned and confess our sins, He is faithful and just (true to His own nature and promises) and will forgive our sins [dismiss our lawlessness] and [continuously] cleanse us from all unrighteousness [everything not in conformity to His will in purpose, thought, and action].

1 JOHN 1:9

five

THE SIMPLICITY OF FORGIVENESS

ne of the biggest obstacles that keeps us from celebrating the life that God has freely bestowed upon us is our own sin consciousness. Sin is a real problem for everyone, but it does not have to be the complicating problem we tend to make it.

That we struggle with our sins is a huge understatement. When we make a mistake, display a weakness, or fail in any way, we often doubt that God loves us, wonder if He is angry at us, try to do all kinds of good works to atone for our failure, and surrender our joy as a sacrifice for our error.

God wants to give us the gift of forgiveness. When we confess our sins to Him, He forgives us of our sins, puts them away from Him as far as the East is from the West, and remembers them no more. But for us to benefit from that forgiveness, we must receive it by faith.

When I was a new believer, each night I would beg God's forgiveness for my past sins. One evening as I knelt beside my bed, I heard Him say, "I forgave you the first time you asked, but you have not received my gift because you have not forgiven yourself."

❧

Jesus bore your sins on the cross, along with the hatred, rejection, and condemnation you deserved. You don't have to reject or hate yourself anymore.

217

GOD'S WORD FOR YOU

My little children, I write you these things so that you may not violate God's law and sin. But if anyone should sin, we have an Advocate (One Who will intercede for us) with the Father—[it is] Jesus Christ [the all] righteous [upright, just, Who conforms to the Father's will in every purpose, thought, and action].

And He [that same Jesus Himself] is the propitiation (the atoning sacrifice) for our sins, and not for ours alone but also for the [sins of] the whole world.

1 JOHN 2:1-2

REE

There was a time in my life when, if you asked me, "What was the last thing you did wrong?" I could have detailed the precise time I had done it and how long I had been paying for it. I worried about every tiny error I made and desperately tried to keep myself from sinning. It was not until I came to comprehend God's forgiveness that I was free from the self-analysis and self-preservation that complicated my life to the extreme.

If you believe that you must be perfect to be worthy of love and acceptance, then you are a candidate for a miserable life because you will never be perfect as long as you are in an earthly body.

You may have a perfect heart, in that your desire is to please God in all things, but your performance will not match your heart's desire until you get to heaven. You can improve all the time and keep pressing toward the mark of perfection, but you will always need Jesus as long as you are here on this earth. There will never come a time when you will not need His forgiveness and cleansing.

God's answer for our imperfection is forgiveness.

GOD'S WORD FOR YOU

For we have not a high priest which cannot be touched with the feeling of our infirmities; but was in all points tempted like as we are, yet without sin.

Let us therefore come boldly unto the throne of grace, that we may obtain mercy, and find grace to help in time of need.

HEBREWS 4:15-16 KJV

JESUS, OUR INTERCESSOR

Jesus *understands* our human frailty because He was tempted in every way that we are, yet without sinning. Therefore, because He is our High Priest, interceding with the Father for us, we can come boldly to God's throne to receive the grace, favor, mercy, and help that we need.

The "good news" is that God has already made provision for every human mistake, weakness, and failure. Salvation and continual forgiveness of our sins are gifts bestowed on us by God because of our acceptance of His Son Jesus Christ. He has forgiven every wrong thing you ever will do!

But Jesus does not want us to use His understanding nature as an excuse to stay in sin that is producing bondage in our lives. He convicts us of sin, but He never condemns us. He brings conviction so that we can see our errors, admit them, be truly sorry, repent, and receive the power of the Holy Spirit. We receive the power or inner strength by asking the Lord to fill us with the Holy Spirit. We can then allow Him to enable us to walk free from the habit that has been sin in our lives.

*Even at our very best, we make mistakes.
To live under condemnation, self-hatred, and self-rejection will not help us live a holier life.*

GOD'S WORD FOR YOU

It is because of the Lord's mercy and loving-kindness that we are not consumed, because His [tender] compassions fail not. [Mal. 3:6.]

They are new every morning; great and abundant is Your stability and faithfulness. [Isa. 33:2.]

LAMENTATIONS 3:22-23

NEW EVERY MORNING

God's mercy is new every morning. Each day we can find a fresh place to begin.

I like the way God has divided up the days and nights. It seems to me that no matter how difficult or challenging a specific day may be, the breaking of dawn brings new hope. God wants us to regularly put the past behind and find a place of "new beginnings."

Perhaps you have been trapped in some sin, and although you have repented, you still feel guilty. You may be assured that sincere repentance brings a fresh, new start because of forgiveness.

Only when you understand the great mercy of God and begin receiving it are you more inclined to give mercy to others. You may be hurting from an emotional wound. The way to put the past behind is to forgive the person who hurt you. Forgiveness is always involved in putting the past behind.

God has new plans on the horizon of your life, but you will never see them if you live in and relive the past. Thinking and talking about the past keeps you trapped in it.

Every day is a new day in God's mercies.
Don't waste today by living in yesterday's sins.

GOD'S WORD FOR YOU

Therefore, [there is] now no condemnation (no adjudging guilty of wrong) for those who are in Christ Jesus, who live [and] walk not after the dictates of the flesh, but after the dictates of the Spirit.

ROMANS 8:1

More Than Enough

Guilt and condemnation are major problems for many believers. Satan's great delight is to make us feel bad about ourselves. He never tells us how far we have come, but rather, he constantly reminds us of how far we still have to go.

When the enemy attacks, say to him, "I'm not where I need to be, but thank God I'm not where I used to be. I'm okay, and I'm on my way."

Like David, we must learn to keep ourselves encouraged in the Lord (1 Samuel 30:6). None of us has arrived at the state of perfection. We cannot perfect ourselves: Sanctification is worked out in our lives by the Holy Spirit as a process.

The Bible teaches that we can have complete forgiveness of our sins (total freedom from condemnation) through the blood of Jesus Christ. We must decide if Jesus did the complete job or if He didn't. We don't need to add our guilt to His sacrifice. He is more than enough.

Let Jesus do His job. He wants to forgive you. All you have to do is receive His forgiveness. Complete forgiveness is completely free!

❧

Don't let the devil fill your head with thoughts of unworthiness as a sinner. Begin to see yourself as the righteousness of God in Christ Jesus.

GOD'S WORD FOR YOU

Blessed (happy, to be envied, and spiritually prosperous—with life-joy and satisfaction in God's favor and salvation, regardless of their outward conditions) are the merciful, for they shall obtain mercy!

MATTHEW 5:7

MERCY EXTENDED

Being merciful can be defined as giving good that is undeserved. Anyone can give people what they deserve. It takes someone full of Jesus to give good to people when they do *not* deserve it.

Revenge says, "You mistreated me, so I'm going to mistreat you." Mercy says, "You mistreated me, so I'm going to forgive you, restore you, and treat you as if you never hurt me." What a blessing to be able to give and receive mercy.

Mercy is an attribute of God's character that is seen in how He deals with His people. Mercy is good to us when we deserve punishment. Mercy accepts and blesses us when we deserve to be totally rejected. Mercy understands our weaknesses and infirmities and does not judge and criticize us.

Do you ever need God or man to show you mercy? Of course, we all do on a regular basis. The best way to get mercy is to be busy giving it away.

Give judgment, and you will receive judgment. Give mercy, and you will receive mercy. You reap what you sow. Be merciful! Be blessed!

Receive God's mercy and love.
You cannot give away something you don't have.

GOD'S WORD FOR YOU

[Now having received the Holy Spirit, and being led and directed by Him] if you forgive the sins of anyone, they are forgiven; if you retain the sins of anyone, they are retained.

JOHN 20:23

. . . forgiving one another [readily and freely], as God in Christ forgave you.

EPHESIANS 4:32

228

KEEP YOUR HEART FREE

When we hold grudges against people, are we really hurting them? Isn't it really ourselves we are hurting?

Jesus frequently spoke of the need to forgive others. If we are to walk His narrow path, we will have to learn to be quick to forgive. The quicker we forgive, the easier it is. We must do it before the problem gets rooted in our emotions. It will be much more difficult to pull out if it has long, strong roots.

Holding grudges against other people does not change them, but it does change us. It makes us sour, bitter, miserable, and difficult to be around. When we think we are holding a grudge, it is actually the grudge that is holding us. It is Satan's deceptive way of keeping us in bondage. He wants us to think we are getting even, that we are protecting ourselves from being hurt again.

None of that is true!

Ask God for grace to forgive anyone against whom you are holding a grudge. Determine from this point on to keep your heart and life free from this negative emotion.

It is impossible to have good emotional health while harboring bitterness, resentment, and unforgiveness. Unforgiveness is poison!

GOD'S WORD FOR YOU

Not that I have now attained [this ideal], or have already been made perfect, but . . . I press on toward the goal to win the [supreme and heavenly] prize to which God in Christ Jesus is calling us upward.

PHILIPPIANS 3:12, 14

Bear (endure, carry) one another's burdens and troublesome moral faults, and in this way fulfill and observe perfectly the law of Christ (the Messiah) and complete what is lacking [in your obedience to it.]

GALATIANS 6:2

TOWARD PERFECTION

"If there is one mark of imperfection, it is simply that it cannot tolerate the imperfections of others." This statement was made by Francois Fenelon in the seventeenth century. When I read that statement, it gripped my heart, and I knew it was something I needed to meditate on.

The apostle Paul stated that he pressed toward the mark of perfection. I believe all those who truly love the Lord are compelled to do that. He is perfect, and our journey into Him compels us to be like Him. We want to do things the right way—the way that brings pleasure to Him.

Perhaps a good measuring stick of our perfection is how patient and forgiving we are with the imperfections of others. When I am impatient with others because of their flaws, if I take a moment and consider my own shortcomings, I usually get patient again very quickly.

If you have an imperfection, don't be down on yourself. God will help you. If you are impatient with the imperfections of others, remember that only imperfection is intolerant of imperfection.

We need to bear one another's weaknesses, realize we all have plenty of them, and pray for one another.

GOD'S WORD FOR YOU

Confess to one another therefore your faults (your slips, your false steps, your offenses, your sins] and pray [also] for one another, that you may be healed and restored [to a spiritual tone of mind and heart]. The earnest (heartfelt, continued) prayer of a righteous man makes tremendous power available [dynamic in its working].

JAMES 5:16

CONFESSION

The passage on confession of sin in James can refer to any kind of sickness—physical, mental, spiritual, and emotional. But does he mean that every time we sin we need to confess it to another person? *No!* With Jesus as our High Priest, we do not need to go to people to receive forgiveness from God.

I believe the time to apply this passage is when you are being tormented by your past sins. Being poisoned inwardly keeps you from getting well and free in that area—physically, mentally, spiritually, or emotionally.

Once exposed to the light, sins hidden in darkness lose their power. People hide sins because of fear as well as pride, and the result is a desperate need that cries out to be released.

The practice of confessing our faults to one another and receiving prayer is a powerful tool to help break bondages. When you find a sin that maintains power over your life, you should prayerfully consider this practice. Seek out a godly person, a Spirit-led confidante, with whom you can share your soul.

It is impossible to allow poison to remain in your soul and get better at the same time!

THE SIMPLICITY OF PRAYER

Pray for what God puts on your heart, not for what everyone else wants to put there.

GOD'S WORD FOR YOU

But you, beloved, build yourselves up [founded] on your most holy faith [make progress, rise like an edifice higher and higher], praying in the Holy Spirit.

JUDE 20

Pray at all times (on every occasion, in every season) in the Spirit, with all [manner of] prayer and entreaty.

EPHESIANS 6:18

six

THE SIMPLICITY OF PRAYER

f you lack real joy in your prayer life, you may discover that you've allowed complexities to smother your approach. I know I did.

My first mistake was in listening to too much of what everyone else said I should be praying about. People told me I should pray about government issues, abortion, Aids, and the homeless. Others gave me a list of missionaries and their specific concerns. Some said I should do spiritual warfare. I was told how long to pray, where to pray, and that the early morning was best.

I converted these instructions into laws I had to do. It was so draining that I finally cried out to God and asked Him to teach me to pray, which is where I should have started in the first place.

He showed me that I would never enjoy prayer if I did not allow Him to lead me. The key was to pray when He was prompting and leading, for the length of time His anointing was present to do so. It was as simple as that.

The secret to a healthy prayer life lies with approaching God simply and gently as a child beloved by the Father.

GOD'S WORD FOR YOU

Is anyone among you afflicted (ill-treated, suffering evil)? He should pray. Is anyone glad at heart? He should sing praise [to God].

Is anyone among you sick? He should call in the church elders (the spiritual guides). And they should pray over him, anointing him with oil in the Lord's name.

And the prayer [that is] of faith will save him who is sick, and the Lord will restore him; and if he has committed sins, he will be forgiven.

JAMES 5:13-15

THE SIMPLE PRAYER OF FAITH

Sometimes when I simply present to God my need or the need of another person, it seems in my "natural man" that I should do or say more. I have found that when I pray what the Holy Spirit is giving me, without adding to it out of my own flesh, the prayer is very simple and not exceedingly long. It requires real discipline on my part to go as far as the Holy Spirit is going and no further.

My mind tells me, "Well, that's not enough, nor is it eloquent enough. And you should pray louder." The flesh generally wants to go beyond what the Spirit is giving us, and that's when we are robbed of the enjoyment that each simple prayer of faith is supposed to bring. We are to say what is on our heart and believe that God has heard us, and that He will take care of it His way, in His timing.

Children are always good examples to follow when searching for simplicity. Listen to a child pray, and it will radically change your prayer life.

Keep prayer simple, and you'll enjoy it more.

GOD'S WORD FOR YOU

Then He was praying in a certain place; and when He stopped, one of His disciples said to Him, Lord, teach us to pray.

LUKE 11:1

BE HONEST WITH GOD

If we are going to spend time in prayer, we want to be certain that our time is well spent, that our prayers are effective, and that we are praying prayers God can answer. We also want to enjoy our prayer time.

A successful prayer life is not developed overnight nor can it be copied from someone else. God has a personal plan for each of us. We cannot always do what someone else is doing and expect it to work for us. Our prayer life is progressive. It progresses as we progress, so be patient!

Often our prayers are too vague, meaning they are not clearly expressed. When you pray, be clear with the Lord. Pray boldly, expectantly, specifically. Your heavenly Father loves you, so come fearlessly, confidently, and boldly to the throne of grace (Hebrews 4:16).

If you need help with your prayer life, be honest with God. Tell Him your needs. He will help you if you ask Him to do so. Begin to say, "Lord, teach me to pray."

We need more confidence in the name of Jesus and less confidence in ourselves or anyone else to solve our problems. There is power in the name of Jesus.

GOD'S WORD FOR YOU

All of you must keep awake (give strict attention, be cautious and active) and watch and pray, that you may not come into temptation. The spirit indeed is willing, but the flesh is weak.

MATTHEW 26:41

242

Watch and Pray

Fear attacks everyone at some time. It is Satan's way of tormenting us and preventing us from going forward so we cannot enjoy the life Jesus died to give us. Fears are not realities. They are **F**alse **E**vidence **A**ppearing **R**eal. But if we accept the fears that Satan offers and give voice to them, we open the door for the enemy and close the door of God.

Satan seeks to weaken us through fear, but God strengthens us as we fellowship with Him in prayer. Faith is released through prayer, which makes tremendous power available, dynamic in its working.

The Bible teaches us to watch and pray. We must watch ourselves and be alert to the attacks the enemy launches against our minds and emotions. When these attacks are detected, we should pray *immediately*. We may think the attack will go away, but we must remember that it is when we pray that power is released against the enemy—not when we think about praying later.

Effectively shutting the door of fear by faith will produce more joy and peace for your everyday living.

Pray about everything and fear nothing.
When fear knocks at the door, let faith answer.

GOD'S WORD FOR YOU

And this is the confidence (the assurance, the privilege of boldness) which we have in Him: [we are sure] that if we ask anything (make any request) according to His will (in agreement with His own plan), He listens to and hears us.

1 JOHN 5:14

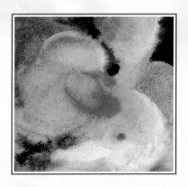

THE CONFIDENCE OF A CHILD

We are to walk in confidence in every area of our lives. Prayer is one of the ways we can show that our confidence is in God. If we pray about everything instead of worrying and trying to work it out ourselves, we say by our attitude and actions, "Lord, I trust You in this situation."

I believe many of us pray and then wonder if God heard. We wonder if we prayed properly or long enough. We wonder if we used the right phrases, enough Scripture, etc. We cannot pray properly with doubt and unbelief. We must pray with faith.

God has been encouraging me to realize that simple faith-filled prayer gets the job done. I don't have to repeat things over and over. I don't need to get fancy in my wording. I can just be me and know that He hears and understands me.

We should simply present our request and believe that God has heard us and will answer at the right time.

Have confidence in your prayers. Believe God hears and is delighted by simple, childlike prayer coming from a sincere heart.

Ask God for what you want and desire, and trust Him to bring it in His way when the time is right.

GOD'S WORD FOR YOU

Be unceasing in prayer [praying perseveringly].

1 THESSALONIANS 5:17

PRAYER IS NOT A BURDEN

If we don't understand simple, believing prayer, the instruction to pray without ceasing can come down on us like a very heavy burden. We may feel that we are doing well to pray thirty minutes a day, so how can we possibly pray without ever stopping? We need such confidence in prayer that it becomes like breathing, an effortless action that we do every moment we are alive. We don't work and struggle at breathing, and neither will we in prayer if we understand its simplicity.

To pray without ceasing does not mean that we must be offering some kind of formal prayer every moment twenty-four hours a day. It means that all throughout the day we should be in a prayerful attitude. As we encounter each situation or as things come to our mind that need attention, we should simply submit them to God in prayer.

We should remember that it is not the length or loudness or eloquence of the prayer that makes it powerful—prayer is made powerful by the sincerity of it and the faith behind it.

We can pray anywhere at anytime about anything. Our prayers can be verbal or silent, long or short, public or private—the important thing is that we pray!

GOD'S WORD FOR YOU

Also when you pray, you must not be like the hypocrites, for they love to pray standing in the synagogues and on the corners of the streets, that they may be seen by people. Truly I tell you, they have their reward in full already.

But when you pray, go into your [most] private room, and, closing the door, pray to your Father, Who is in secret; and your Father, Who sees in secret, will reward you in the open.

MATTHEW 6:5-6

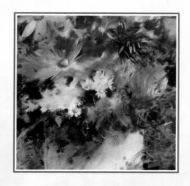

SECRET PRAYER

Although some prayers are public prayers or group prayers, most of our prayer life is secret and should be kept that way. "Secret prayer" means that we don't tell everyone we know about our personal experiences in prayer and how much we pray. We pray about the concerns and people God places on our heart, and we keep our prayers between us and Him unless we have a really good reason to do otherwise. We refuse to make a display of our prayers to impress others as the hypocritical Pharisee did in Luke 18:10-14.

For prayer to be properly called "secret prayer," it must come from a humble heart as was demonstrated in the prayer of the despised tax collector. He humbled himself, bowed his head, and quietly, with humility, asked God to forgive him. In response to his sincerity, a lifetime of sin was wiped away in a moment.

God has not given us a bunch of complicated, hard-to-follow guidelines. Christianity is simple until complicated people make it complicated.

*Believing prayer is not possible
if we base the value of our prayers on feelings.*

GOD'S WORD FOR YOU

*Keep on asking and it will be given you; keep on
seeking and you will find; keep on knocking [reverently]
and [the door] will be opened to you.*

*For everyone who keeps on asking receives; and he
who keeps on seeking finds; and to him who keeps on
knocking, [the door] will be opened.*

MATTHEW 7:7-8

PERSISTENCE IN PRAYER

It is difficult to lay down any strict rules on how often to pray about the same concern. Some people say, "Pray repeatedly until you see the breakthrough." Others say, "If you pray more than once, you didn't believe you got it the first time."

Sometimes when we ask God the same thing over and over, it is a sign of doubt and unbelief, not of faith and persistence. It is like the dynamic that occurs when our own children make a request of us and come back an hour later and ask again.

When I ask the Lord for something in prayer, and that matter comes to my mind or heart again later, I talk to Him about it. But when I do, I refrain from asking Him the same thing. I thank Him that He is working on the situation, but I don't repray the same prayer all over again.

Jesus' admonition is persistence not repetition. We should keep pressing on and never give up—if we are sure we are pursuing the will of God. Persistent prayer builds even more faith and confidence as we pray. The stronger our confidence is, the better off we are.

Believe that God delights in your prayers and is ready to answer any request that is in accordance with His will. Come as a believer, not a beggar.

251

JOYCE MEYER

JOYCE MEYER has been teaching the Word of God
since 1976 and in full-time ministry since 1980.
She is the bestselling author of more than sixty
inspirational books, including *In Pursuit of Peace*,
How to Hear from God, *Knowing God Intimately*, and
Battlefield of the Mind. She has also released thousands
of teaching cassettes and a complete video library.
Joyce's *Enjoying Everyday Life* radio and television
programs are broadcast around the world, and she
travels extensively conducting conferences. Joyce and
her husband, Dave, are the parents of four grown
children and make their home in St. Louis, Missouri.

Additional copies of this book are available from your local bookstore.

If this book has changed your life, we would like to hear from you.

Please write us at:

Joyce Meyer Ministries
P.O. Box 655 • Fenton, MO 63026

or call: (636) 349-0303

Internet Address: www.joycemeyer.org

In Canada, write: Joyce Meyer Ministries Canada, Inc.
Lambeth Box 1300 • London, ON N6P 1T5

or call: (636) 349-0303

In Australia, write: Joyce Meyer Ministries—Australia
Locked Bag 77 • Mansfield Delivery Centre
Queensland 4122

or call: (07) 3349 1200

In England, write: Joyce Meyer Ministries
P.O. Box 1549 • Windsor • SL4 1GT

or call: 01753 831102